AF879300

STORYBUILDING

YOUR BRAND FROM THEIR STANDPOINT

CUSTOMER, USER, INVESTOR, DONOR, PARTNER, SUPPLIER, BOSS

JOHN ELBING

SIGN UP FOR THE EXTRA CONTENT

Flash the QR code to sign up, and start with ***downloading all the canvases****.*

All the Canvases

Secret Reader Access Code

PaleBlueDot

This book is for you

If you are

- An Entrepreneur
- A Business Owner
- In Marketing
- In Sales
- In Product Development
- In Project Management
- In Customer Support
- Working for a Non-Profit
- Looking for Donors
- Wanting to convince your Boss… or Partner
- Curious about the difference between storytelling and Storybuilding

Because

You will

- Unlock powerful insights about your customers.
- Master the art of crafting stories that truly connect with them.
- Realign your positioning to resonate where it matters most.
- Bask in your success.

Storybuilding – Your Brand From Their Standpoint

Copyright ©2025 John Elbing

All Rights Reserved. No part of this book may be reproduced, distributed, or transmitted in any form or by any means, including photocopying, recording, or other electronic or mechanical methods, without the prior written permission of the publisher, except in the case of brief quotations in reviews.

Publishing:

Epic Author Publishing

support@epicauthor.com - www.epicauthor.com

Cover design, illustrations, and layout:

By tucity   tucitydesign@gmail.com

ISBNs:

Paperback: 978-1-947276-65-9

eBook: 978-1-947276-64-2

First Edition: April 2025

Printed in U.S.A.

For bulk orders, interviews, or speaking engagements, visit:

standpoint.ch/storybuilding-book

To my exceptional daughter,
my wonderful partner,
and my fluffy cat.

TABLE OF CONTENTS

PART 1: THE BIG WHY 1

This isn't just about marketing - it's about making your brand connect, stand out, and stick. A secret weapon for realignment and engagement, with extra content, tools, and a community to back you up.

01 WHAT IS STORYBUILDING 3

This book is for you. How will it make your life better?

02 WHY STORYBUILDING REALLY MATTERS 9

The Trojan Horse of Brand Realignment

03 THIS BOOK IS INTERACTIVE 19

Become a member of the Storybuilding Community & get extra content

PART 2: ENCOUNTERING A BRAND 25

Customers encounter a brand in 3 steps: ***Recognition*** *(Is this for me?),* ***Perception*** *(Do I get it?), and* ***Projection*** *(Will this improve my life?). Get them right, and they're in—get them wrong, and they're gone. Let's make sure they stay.*

04 RECOGNITION 31

Do they work with people/companies like me?

05 PERCEPTION 47

How are they different? What do I compare them to? Is their offer clear?

06 PROJECTION 55

What will it be like? How will my life be better?

07 SELF-CENTERED BRANDS 61

What happens when brands don't take their customers' standpoint, and only talk about themselves, about what they do?

PART 3: UNDERSTANDING 69

To tell a story that sticks, you need to see the world through the eyes of your customer (or investor, or boss). What do they want? What do they feel? Then, flip the lens on your own brand—because sometimes, the outside view is way more revealing than the inside one. Time to sharpen your focus!

08 PRACTICAL TIPS 71

Team of customer facing people. White board and sticky notes.

09 YOUR STAKEHOLDERS (CUSTOMERS) 77

Who are your customers, and what are their aspirations and their challenges?

A. SIDE QUEST: TRIGGER MARKETING 101

10 YOUR ORGANIZATION (COMPANY) 107

Take a hard look on your organization.

B. SIDE QUEST: YOUR CATEGORY 141

PART 4: STORYBUILDING 147

Now that you know what matters, it's time to craft a story that actually works. We'll map out the structure, shape the narrative, and make sure it's told from the right perspective - theirs. By the end, your brand won't just talk; it'll resonate.

11 STORYBUILDING FRAMEWORK 149

Decide what is important and put the pieces in an engaging sequence.

12 TEST IF IT'S THE RIGHT STORY 179

Confront the world with your story, first by comparing to competing stories.

C. SIDE QUEST: YOUR COMPETITORS' POSITIONING 185

13 THE STORY 191

You have the sequence, time to make it into a story.

D. SIDE QUEST: YOUR TAGLINE 205

PART 5: HOW YOU WILL USE IT 209

Your story isn't one-size-fits-all—it adapts. Whether for different audiences, channels, or business cases, Storybuilding flexes to fit. In this section, we'll explore how to apply it effectively and see it in action.

14 WHAT AND WHERE 211

Let's explore…

15 TYPES OF APPLICATION 217

Pretty much anywhere

E. SIDE QUEST: YOUR OFFER 221

16 B2C-BUSINESS TO CONSUMER 231

The most obvious usage is for B2C companies.

17 CASE STUDY: FELCO 239

The world leader in garden shears needed to contrast their three brands

18 B2B-BUSINESS TO BUSINESS 245

It is just as powerful with B2B companies

19 NON-PROFIT 253

Non-profits are still "selling" something

20 MARKETPLACE 261

A little twist when there are two customers

21 INVESTOR 271

You "sell" your idea to an investor

22 INTERNAL PROJECT PITCH 277

You can also convince your boss of your great idea

PART 6: CONCLUSION 283

We've built your story, sharpened your message, and reimagined your brand. Now it's time to put it all into action. So, is this goodbye? Not quite—your story is just getting started.

23 WRAP UP 285

This is what you have learned

24 ACKNOWLEDGMENTS 293

Thank you all so much

25 ABOUT THE AUTHOR 295

John Elbing

26 EPILOGUE 299

Where did this book come from?

PART 1:
THE BIG WHY

This isn't just about marketing - it's about making your brand connect, stand out, and stick. A secret weapon for realignment and engagement, with extra content, tools, and a community to back you up.

WHAT IS STORYBUILDING 01

This book is for you. How will it make your life better?

Picture yourself at a dinner party. One guest won't stop talking about themselves—their awards, their genius ideas, their latest life-changing vacation (that you definitely did not ask about). Another actually asks about you—what you do, what you care about, maybe even laughs at your jokes. Who would you rather be stuck next to when dessert takes forever? No contest. We connect with people who make us feel seen, heard and understood.

Storybuilding is about making your brand that good conversationalist—the one that listens, understands, and makes people feel seen. It's not about shouting your message into the void; it's about crafting a story that fits into your audience's world, their challenges, and what actually matters to them. Whether you're talking to customers, investors, or that donor who still isn't sure about you, the secret isn't what you want to say—it's what they need to hear.

It's the art of positioning your brand from *their* standpoint.

IS THIS BOOK FOR YOU?

Let's do a quick test. If any of these sound like you, keep reading. If not... well, keep reading anyway. You might surprise yourself.

- You're an **entrepreneur** trying to attract loyal customers but often feel like you're screaming into the void.
- A **marketer** desperate for engagement but mostly getting polite nods (or worse, complete silence).
- A **sales professional** who wants to connect meaningfully but ends up hearing, "Let me think about it" way too often.
- A **leader** persuading people to believe in their vision but getting more blank stares than enthusiasm.
- Or simply someone who's curious about how stories can work magic in business - and wouldn't mind having a superpower that actually gets people to listen.

If you've ever struggled to make your brand stand out in a sea of sameness, found yourself explaining your product over and over with no lightbulb moment on the other end, or felt like your message was about as clear as a foggy car windshield, then congratulations! This book is your defogger.

By the time you're done, you'll know exactly how to tell a story that makes your audience lean in, not tune out. And if that's not useful, I don't know what is.

THE PROMISE OF STORYBUILDING

Storytelling is powerful, but Storybuilding takes it a step further. Instead of focusing on what you want to say, it starts with what your audience needs to hear. The difference? One is like a pushy salesperson who won't let you leave without buying something. The other is like a trusted friend who actually listens before offering advice (and maybe even buys you a coffee first). Which one would you rather engage with?

With Storybuilding, you will:

- **Understand your audience's mindset** - what they want, what frustrates them, and what actually drives their decisions (hint: it's often coffee and deadlines).
- **Craft stories that resonate** - not just catchy marketing slogans, but narratives that genuinely connect (and don't make people roll their eyes).
- **Make your brand more relevant and memorable** - because people remember stories that feel like they belong to them (not just ones that sound like corporate jargon bingo).
- **Unlock new opportunities** - when people feel understood, they trust you, and trust leads to action (and maybe even brand loyalty).

HOW THIS BOOK WILL GUIDE YOU

We'll take you step by step through the Storybuilding process:

- **Recognition:** What do people see, feel, and think when they encounter your brand? Do they immediately recognize it as relevant to them, or do they just blink and scroll away?
- **Perception:** Are you different? How do they compare you to alternatives? Is your offer clear, credible, and aligned with what they actually need, or are you lost in a sea of sameness?
- **Projection:** What happens next? What will their experience be like if they choose you? Can they see how their life or work will improve, or does your offer leave them more confused than before?

These steps will become your foundation. Using canvases, frameworks, and real-world examples, you'll map out the journey from understanding your audience to crafting a story they embrace.

THE METHOD: A SIMPLE ROADMAP

Here's how we'll bring Storybuilding to life:

- **Step 1: Stakeholder Canvas** – First, we'll get into your audience's head. What do they want? What's holding them back? What shapes their decisions? (No, you don't need to be a mind reader, but close.)
- **Step 2: Organization Canvas** – Next, we'll turn the lens on you. How does your brand actually help? What makes you different? What's the experience like? (And if you say "we're just better," we're going to need to dig deeper.)
- **Step 3: Storybuilding Canvas** – Now, we start building. You'll decide what matters most and arrange the pieces into a compelling sequence. Think of it as putting together a puzzle—except you get to choose the picture on the box.
- **Step 4: Story Canvas** – Finally, we'll bring it all together into a fully formed brand story that speaks directly to your audience (without making them snore).

By the end, you won't just have a great marketing story—you'll have a strategy that makes your brand more relevant, more trusted, and more successful (and possibly the life of the metaphorical dinner party).

A BETTER FUTURE FOR YOUR BRAND

Embracing Storybuilding isn't just about crafting better marketing messages—it's about building **trust, loyalty, and real emotional connections**. When you do it right, your brand stops being just another option. It becomes **the obvious choice**.

So, let's stop just telling stories. Let's build stories that belong to your audience. And in doing so, let's make them want to engage with you (and maybe even tell their friends about you).

Ready? Let's get started.

Actually, before we get started, let me tell you why Storybuilding really matters.

STORYBUILDING
N
W
E
S

WHY STORYBUILDING REALLY MATTERS 02

The Trojan Horse of Brand Realignment

You might be thinking, "Is this just another marketing book telling me to 'tell better stories'?" Nope. Storybuilding isn't about slapping together a feel-good brand tale with a catchy tagline. It's about realigning your brand—without making it feel like a corporate existential crisis.

Here's the truth: when companies embrace Storybuilding, the impact goes way beyond marketing. It forces them to take a good, hard look at themselves (*cue dramatic mirror scene*), their customers, and their actual place in the market. And guess what? That's when the magic happens.

Most businesses struggle with one of these three things:

- They **talk about themselves** too much (news flash: nobody cares about your origin story unless it's relevant).
- They **assume** customers automatically **understand** their value (*spoiler: they don't*).
- Their messaging is so **generic** it could be copied and pasted onto any competitor's website (*"We are innovative, customer-focused, and passionate"*—wow, groundbreaking).

Storybuilding fixes all of this by flipping the script. Instead of focusing on what you want to say, it starts with what your audience actually needs to hear. It's like going from bad small talk at a networking event to a deep, engaging conversation over drinks.

And the best part? It sneaks in a brand realignment without triggering corporate resistance. That's why I call it *the Trojan Horse of brand strategy*. It looks like a simple storytelling method, but inside, it's packed with powerful insights that reshape how you position yourself, communicate your value, and connect with customers.

THE STORYBUILDING PROCESS (HOW YOU STOP BEING IGNORED)

At its core, Storybuilding is a structured way to make your brand impossible to ignore. Here's how it works:

- **Step into your audience's mind** – What do they really care about? What keeps them up at night? What words would they actually use to describe their problem? (Hint: It's rarely "I need a scalable, AI-powered solution.")
- **Take a brutally honest look at your brand** – Do you actually solve those problems, or are you just assuming you do? (*Be honest, this is a safe space.*)
- **Align your message with what they need to hear** – This is where you stop saying "We are the best" and start saying, "Here's how your life will be better with us in it."
- **Build an engaging story** – One that doesn't just inform but makes people *feel* something. (*And no, not just boredom.*)

This process forces you to ask the tough questions:

- Are we actually serving our customers the way we think we are?
- Are we making it painfully clear why we're the best choice?
- Are we positioning ourselves in a way that makes competitors irrelevant?

If you haven't asked these before, congrats—you're about to unlock game-changing clarity.

THE UNEXPECTED BENEFITS OF STORYBUILDING

Storybuilding isn't just about better marketing. It delivers massive benefits that ripple across your business.

Sharper Focus (Stop Trying to Be Everything to Everyone)

Storybuilding helps you get crystal clear on what really matters. You'll finally ditch the fluff and focus on:

- Who your best customers are (not just anyone with a credit card).
- What they actually want (not what you wish they wanted).
- How to communicate your value in a way that clicks instantly.

The result? You stop wasting time on messaging that doesn't work and start attracting the right people.

Stronger Alignment (Getting Everyone to Actually Agree on Something)

If your marketing team says one thing, your sales team says another, and your CEO is off on a TED Talk tangent about "synergy," then you have an alignment problem. Storybuilding gets everyone singing the same song by answering:

- Who are we really for?
- What problem do we solve better than anyone else?
- What should every customer-facing person say when asked, "Why should I choose you?"

When you nail this, your team stops sounding like a chaotic jazz band and starts hitting all the right notes.

Strategic Adjustments (The Moment You Realize You Need to Change Something)

Storybuilding often uncovers some tough truths—like maybe you're marketing to the wrong people, or your messaging is as clear as a cryptic fortune cookie. But that's a good thing! Because now you can make *smart* adjustments, like:

- **Narrowing your focus** – Instead of appealing to *everyone*, you laser in on the people who actually care. (*Because let's be honest, not everyone cares.*)
- **Restructuring your offer** – Maybe customers love part of your product but ignore the rest. Time to tweak the packaging (*figuratively or literally*).
- **Repositioning against competitors** – If you're constantly being compared to another brand, why not shift the playing field so you're the obvious choice?

True Customer-Centricity (Actually Putting Customers First Instead of Just Saying You Do)

Most businesses say they're customer-centric, but their messaging says otherwise. If your website is all about you instead of them, you've already lost.

Storybuilding forces you to take the customer's standpoint so that:

- You create messages that make people say, "Wow, they get me."
- Your marketing stops being an infomercial and starts feeling like a helpful conversation.
- You build trust, loyalty, and—most importantly—actual sales.

A Competitive Edge
(Why You'll Stop Being a Forgettable Option")

Differentiation isn't just about having the best product. It's about *owning the narrative.* With Storybuilding, you:

- Highlight what makes you *truly* unique (*not just "great customer service"*—everyone says that).
- Position yourself as the brand that *understands* your audience better than anyone else.
- Create emotional connections that make price a secondary concern. (*Because if they love your brand, they'll pay more for it.*)

CASE STUDIES: WHEN STORYBUILDING CHANGES EVERYTHING

Example 1: The Startup That Finally Found Its Niche

A software company was struggling to gain traction. Their website was a feature dump, and their pitch was: "We help businesses manage projects efficiently." (*Groundbreaking.*)

After applying Storybuilding, they realized small business teams needed *simplicity,* not complexity. They rebranded as "The Easiest Project Management Tool for Small Teams" and BOOM 40 percent growth in a year.

Example 2: The Non-Profit That Stopped Sounding Boring

A non-profit was struggling to attract donors because their messaging was all about *them.* Using Storybuilding, they flipped the *focus to the impact donors could have*—and their donor retention shot up by 25 percent.

Example 3: The Company That Finally Made Customers Care

A B2B brand selling security software kept talking about "enterprise-grade encryption." (*Yawn.*) After Storybuilding, they repositioned as "The Only Cybersecurity System Built for Non-Tech People." Sales skyrocketed.

WHY STORYBUILDING IS WORTH IT

At the end of the day, this isn't just about crafting a better story—it's about making your business impossible to ignore.

If you want to:

- Stand out in a crowded market
- Create messaging that actually resonates
- Get customers to say "*This is exactly what I need!*"

Then it's time to embrace Storybuilding.

Are you ready? Let's flip your brand's perspective and make your audience the hero.

SIDE QUESTS

Because Every Hero Needs Extra Loot

These aren't mandatory, but skipping them is like ignoring free snacks at a party. Why would you do that?

- **Trigger Marketing:** Catch customers *at the perfect moment*—right when they're thinking, *"Hey, I need that!"* It's like showing up with an umbrella *right* before it rains.
- **Define Your Category:** Why fight to be the best when you can just be the *only*? Different is better than better—because better is debatable, but different *owns the game.*
- **Tagline Templates:** If people start using your tagline in casual conversation, *congrats, you've won marketing.* These templates help make it happen.
- **Compare Competing Stories:** If your brand story were in a talent show against competitors, would it get a standing ovation or polite golf claps? Let's make sure *you're the headliner.*
- **Good, Better, Best Pricing:** Give customers options without making them overthink. Based on the four levers of value perception (*which sounds fancy but is actually just good strategy*).

Choose your side quest wisely—or better yet, do them all. Because who doesn't want extra XP?

Sellers
Buyers
STORY
TELLING

THIS BOOK IS INTERACTIVE 03

Become a member of the Storybuilding Community & get extra content

DON'T JUST READ – BUILD SOMETHING

Most books are passive—you read them, take some notes, and move on.

Not this one.

This book is meant to be **used**. By the time you finish, you won't just have insights about storytelling—you'll have built a compelling brand story that **connects with your audience** and **strengthens your positioning**.

To get there, you'll engage with **exercises, digital tools, community discussions, and AI-powered thinking prompts**.

Let's unlock them together.

HOW TO USE THIS BOOK

Think of this book like a **workshop in print**—a mix of theory, practical exercises, and interactive experiences.

Here's what you'll find:

- **Exercises & Templates** – Apply the concepts directly to your business.
- **Hidden Bonuses** – QR codes unlock **videos, examples, resources, and tools**.
- **AI Assistance** – Pre-built AI prompts help you brainstorm and refine your ideas.
- **Community** – Share insights, ask questions, and get feedback.

Find Hidden Gems

Throughout the book, you'll find **QR codes**. Think of them as **treasure chests** - scan them to unlock bonus content like:

- Videos that dive deeper into key concepts
- Downloadable worksheets & canvases
- Surprise insights you won't find in print
- "Ask AI" prompts

AI as Your Thinking Partner

AI won't replace your creativity, but it can help you **brainstorm, refine, and challenge your thinking**.

When you see "**Ask AI**" sidebars, snap the QR code and grab pre-built questions you can copy, paste, and adapt with your favorite AI chatbot.

These prompts will help you brainstorm more ideas, faster. You will get a brutally honest view on your progress.

Warning: AI tends to be overly polite. Some prompts will push it to be **brutally honest**—even **mean**—to help you **refine your messaging**.

JOIN THE STORYBUILDING COMMUNITY

Great ideas don't grow in isolation.

The first time you will scan a QR code, you will join the Storybuilding Community, where you can:

- Discuss exercises and share insights
- Ask questions and get feedback
- See how others are crafting their stories

▶ *Community Sign Up*

Secret Reader Access Code
PaleBlueDot

Depending on when you're reading this, the community may be **just getting started**—or it may already be a **thriving hub of insights**. Either way, you're invited.

FIRST QUEST

Let's give it a try.

Try this first AI prompt!

▶ *First AI Prompt*

This book is meant to be experienced, not just read.

Let's dive in.

What goes through people's heads when they encounter a brand?

By understanding how your customer thinks, you can better connect with them—by telling their story.

Want the deep dive? Keep reading.

Impatient? Adventurous? Go ahead and jump straight to the exercises on page 69. We won't judge.

PART 2: ENCOUNTERING A BRAND

Customers encounter a brand in 3 steps: ***Recognition*** *(Is this for me?),* ***Perception*** *(Do I get it?), and* ***Projection*** *(Will this improve my life?). Get them right, and they're in—get them wrong, and they're gone. Let's make sure they stay.*

The Situation

Every time we encounter a brand, our brains go through a predictable routine—like an autopilot mode for decision-making.

There's a person. They have an identity—shaped by personality, habits, beliefs, personal circumstances, and professional roles. They have dreams, frustrations, and a never-ending to-do list.

Then, they encounter a brand.

Maybe they walk into a store. Maybe they land on a website. Maybe they see an ad on their way to work and wonder, "Do I need that?"

Within seconds, they react. And believe it or not, it's not random. There's a pattern to it.

Encountering a Brand

Whether it's a company, a product, or even a personal brand, we all go through the same subconscious process when we come across something new.

It happens fast—so fast that by the time a brand realizes you've seen them, you may have already decided whether you care. If businesses understood this process better, they'd stop losing customers before the conversation even starts.

This part of the book unpacks what happens when people encounter a brand. It boils down to three key steps:

1. **Recognition** – "Is this for me? Do they work with people like me?"
2. **Perception** – "Do I get what they offer? How are they different?"
3. **Projection** – "What would it be like to buy from them? Will my life be better?"

Master these three steps, and you won't just grab attention—you'll hold onto it. And in the fast-paced world of modern business, that's the difference between a customer clicking away and a customer clicking 'buy.'

Let's take a closer look inside your audience's mind when they first meet your brand. Because once you understand how they think, you can tell a story that doesn't just reach them—it pulls them in and keeps them engaged.

Beyond Just Customers

This process isn't just about marketing—it's about persuasion in any setting.

Every time you present an idea, make a pitch, or ask for something, you're making a proposal. And the person on the receiving end is going through the same mental process:

- A customer evaluates a brand's offer.
- A user judges an app or a product.
- An investor weighs a startup pitch.
- A donor decides whether to contribute.
- A business partner considers a collaboration.
- A supplier reviews an RFP.
- Your boss debates approving your project.
- Your partner contemplates your vacation idea (hint: make it sound relaxing *and* adventurous).

For simplicity, we'll focus on customers and brands. But remember, this framework applies to countless interactions in business and life.

Master it, and you'll not only sell better—you'll communicate better, persuade better, and, let's be honest, probably win more arguments at home too.

YOUR BRAND

RECOGNITION 04

Do they work with people/companies like me?

Back to our individual.

Our brains are lazy. The moment we see a brand, we make a snap judgment: "Is this for me, or should I keep scrolling/walking/sprinting away like it's a *robocall about my car's extended warranty*?"

Our first reaction to a brand often starts with a gut feeling: "Is this for me?"

Your brain doesn't *analyze*—it *feels.* It's the same reason you can immediately tell whether a party is going to be fun or if you should start crafting an excuse to leave. Recognition isn't logic; it's vibes.

This decision happens quickly. When you pass a store window or restaurant, you instinctively know whether you want to stop and look closer. Similarly, when you click on a website, you decide within seconds whether to keep reading or move on.

In those moments, you subconsciously ask questions like:

- Do they work with people like me?
- Do they understand what I want to accomplish?
- Do they know the challenges I face?

If a brand doesn't get this right, you're out before they even know you were there. It's like a bad first date—if the vibe is off in the first five minutes, there's no way you're sticking around for dessert.

Any hesitation or disconnect in these answers can turn you away—before you've even analyzed their offer.

This step is very emotional.

EXAMPLES OF FIRST IMPRESSIONS

Scenario 1: Coffee with a Friend

You're looking for a place for your caffeine fix. You pass by:

- **A cozy café** with a chalkboard menu and a barista who *definitely* has a novel in the works.
- **A tearoom** where they serve tiny sandwiches and judge you for asking for extra sugar.
- **A biker bar** where the coffee is black, the mugs are heavier than your gym weights, and asking for oat milk might get you kicked out.
- **A trendy coffee shop** where the Wi-Fi is strong, but so is the pressure to order something with turmeric.

What draws you in depends on:

- **Who you are:** Are you a neighborhood regular, someone who loves elegance, a thrill-seeker, or part of the cool crowd?
- **What you want:** Do you need a simple transaction, a quiet conversation, a good laugh, or just your favorite coffee?
- **Your challenges:** Do you want to avoid overthinking, feel accepted, avoid behaving a certain way, or ensure there's Wi-Fi?

Within seconds, your decision is clear.

Some cues—like elegant patrons—are obvious. Others, such as knowing a trendy café likely has Wi-Fi, come from experience.

Scenario 2: Shopping for Clothes

You need a new outfit. Maybe for a big event, maybe because your favorite jeans finally gave up, or maybe just because retail therapy is cheaper than actual therapy (sort of). You pass by:

- **A secondhand shop** – where every rack is a treasure hunt, and you might score designer for the price of a sandwich.
- **A department store** – where you could find what you need… if only you could survive the endless aisles and that one overly enthusiastic perfume sprayer.
- **A children's clothing store** – where everything is tiny and adorable, but unless you're shopping for a toddler, it's not your stop.
- **A luxury boutique** – where the price tags have more zeroes than your bank account, but the lighting makes you feel like a fashion icon.

Tees
Shirts

GIRLS

LOUIS VUITTON

Your choice depends on:

- **Who you are:** Are you an eco-conscious thrifter, a practical shopper, a fashion risk-taker, or just here because your mom said you needed a new jacket?
- **What you want:** A budget-friendly find, a staple piece that goes with everything, a bold new look, or a splurge that makes you feel like royalty?
- **Your challenges:** Avoiding buyer's remorse, finding something that actually fits and looks good, navigating confusing sizing charts, or resisting the urge to buy yet another black T-shirt?

Recognition happens in seconds. The moment you see a store, your brain already knows: "*Yes, this is my vibe*" or "*Nope, I'll stick to online shopping*".

They will attract the right kind of customer and avoid attracting the wrong kind.

Scenario 3: Choosing a To-Do App

You've finally accepted that keeping your to-do list in your head is *not* a reliable strategy. It's time to get an app—something that will keep you on track, boost your productivity, and maybe, just maybe, stop you from forgetting birthdays. You start browsing and see:

- **The Teamwork Titan** – Promises seamless collaboration, real-time syncing, and enough features to make you feel like you're running a Fortune 500 company—even if it's just you and your cat.
- **The Grocery Guru** – Focused on meal planning, shopping lists, and making sure you never forget to buy milk again (even though you will).
- **The Workflow Warrior** – Marketed to high-achievers with color-coded dashboards, automated reminders, and productivity stats that will either inspire you or give you anxiety.
- **The Zen Planner** – More about mindfulness than deadlines. Uses soothing colors and gentle nudges like "Take a deep breath. You've got this." Meanwhile, your actual tasks are still waiting.

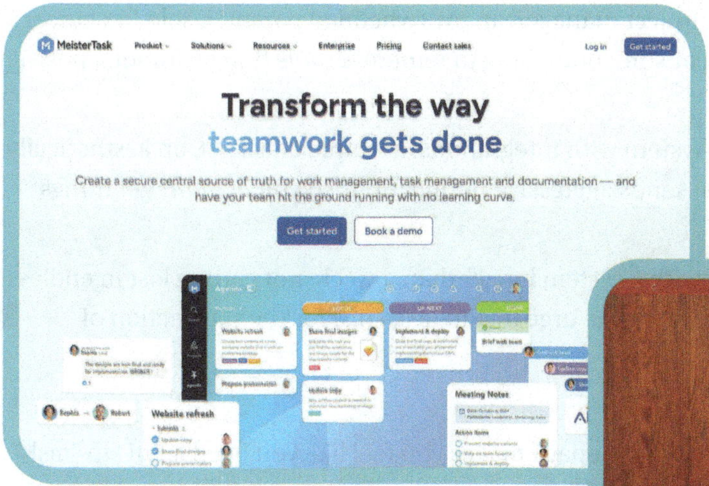
MeisterTask
Product
Solutions
Resources
Enterprise
Pricing
Contact sales
Log in
Get started
Transform the way
teamwork gets done
Create a secure central source of truth for work management, task management and documentation — and have your team hit the ground running with no learning curve.
Get started
Book a demo
Website refresh
Meeting Notes

Today
pickup stuff for guac!
Your Life in Lists
Clear is a colorful canvas for your thoughts, plans and goals. Here's what makes it uniquely fun and effective.

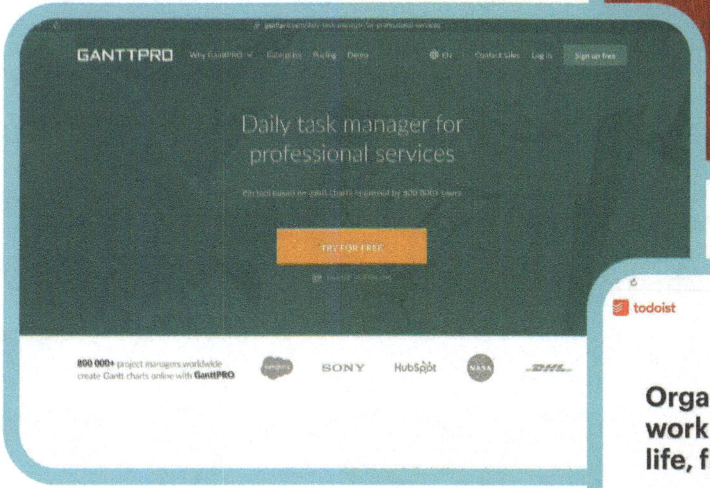
GANTTPRO
Sign up free
Daily task manager for professional services
TRY FOR FREE
800 000+ project managers worldwide create Gantt charts online with GanttPRO
SONY
HubSpot
NASA
DHL

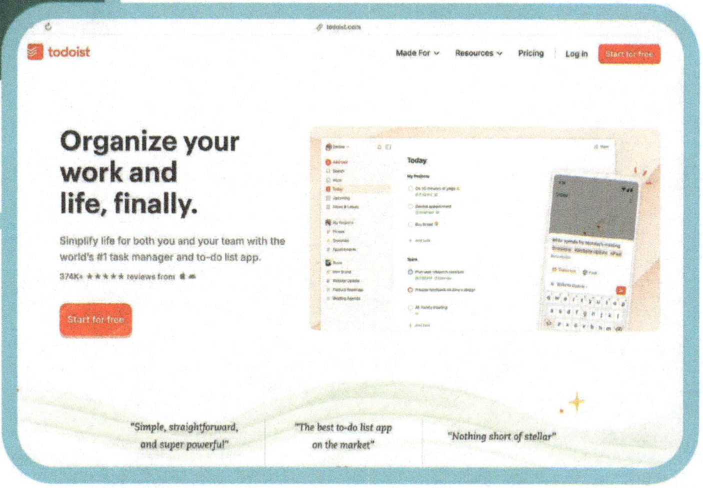
todoist.com
todoist
Made For
Resources
Pricing
Log in
Start for free
Organize your work and life, finally.
Simplify life for both you and your team with the world's #1 task manager and to-do list app.
374K+ ★★★★★ reviews from
Start for free
Today
"Simple, straightforward, and super powerful"
"The best to-do list app on the market"
"Nothing short of stellar"

Your choice depends on:

- **Who you are:** A hardcore project manager, an overwhelmed parent, a solo freelancer juggling too many clients, or someone trying to remember *one* thing without a post-it note?
- **What you want:** A robust system with integrations, a simple checklist, an aesthetically pleasing UI, or an app that sends aggressive notifications so you *actually* get things done?
- **Your challenges:** Sticking with a system longer than a week, not getting lost in endless customization options, resisting the urge to add tasks *just* for the satisfaction of checking them off.

The decision happens fast. If an app's homepage makes you feel like you need a PhD in "task management theory" to use it, you're out. If it shows exactly what you need in a clear, relatable way—you're in.

OTHER SCENARIOS

Investor

You've got some money to invest, and while you'd love to just hide it under your mattress, you decide to be *smart* about it. So, you start looking at options:

- **A mutual fund** – Boring but (mostly) safe. Feels like eating your vegetables—you know it's good for you, but it's not exactly thrilling.
- **A hot new startup** – The founders claim they're "disrupting the industry," but mostly, they're burning through cash like it's a bonfire.
- **Your sister's organic bakery** – She swears it'll be the next big thing… as soon as she figures out how to turn a profit.
- **Crypto** – High risk, high reward, and high chance you'll be explaining your decision to your accountant with a deep sense of regret.

Your choice depends on:

- **Who you are:** A cautious planner, a thrill-seeker, a supportive family member, or someone just trying to sound impressive at dinner parties.
- **What you want:** Steady growth, a big win, bragging rights, or simply to sleep at night without worrying about market crashes.
- **Your challenges:** Understanding risk, avoiding FOMO, or resisting bad financial advice from that one guy at the gym.

Within seconds, you recognize whether an investment aligns with your goals or feels like a money pit.

Donor

You want to donate to a good cause, but there are *so many options.* Where do you start?

- **Humanitarian relief** – Urgent, important, and life-changing… but do you trust the organization, or is it one of those where 90 percent of the funds go to "administrative costs"?
- **Environmental causes** – You want to save the planet, but is planting a tree enough to undo your online shopping addiction?
- **Local community programs** – Helping people in your own city feels great, but you wonder if it's enough of an impact.
- **A viral GoFundMe** – Someone's dog needs surgery, and suddenly, it feels like your responsibility.

Your choice depends on:

- **Who you are:** A strategic philanthropist, a "give where it feels right" kind of person, or someone who just wants to avoid guilt.
- **What you want:** Maximum impact, emotional satisfaction, good PR, or simply to feel like you've done something meaningful.
- **Your challenges:** Trusting organizations, picking between equally worthy causes, or not feeling guilty about saying no to the tenth fundraising email this week.

Before even clicking "Donate," you recognize if the cause speaks to you—or if it's just good marketing.

Boss

You're the boss, and your team keeps pitching new projects. Some are brilliant. Others? Not so much.

- **The cost-cutting initiative** – Promises to save money, but probably means you'll have a very cranky staff.
- **The bold new product launch** – Could be the next big thing… or the next big flop.
- **The "innovative" workflow system** – A fancy way of saying more meetings and software nobody wants to learn.
- **The team-building retreat** – Sounds great until you realize it involves trust falls and awkward icebreakers.

Your choice depends on:

- **Who you are:** A visionary leader, a numbers-driven exec, or someone who just wants to keep things running smoothly.
- **What you want:** Innovation, stability, cost savings, or to be seen as a leader who "gets things done."
- **Your challenges:** Avoiding wasted budgets, making decisions that actually move the needle, or not laughing when someone suggests yet another "AI-powered solution."

If the pitch doesn't align with your priorities, it's a no—no matter how many fancy slides are in the presentation.

Sweetheart: The Vacation Debate

You and your partner are planning a vacation. You'd think this would be exciting, but it quickly turns into a diplomatic negotiation.

- **A beach getaway** – Relaxing, sunny, and involves doing *absolutely nothing.* Perfect, unless one of you gets bored easily.
- **A European city tour** – Culture, history, and walking. *A lot of* walking. You might need a second vacation to recover.
- **An adventurous trek** – Stunning views, thrilling experiences, and a high probability of sore muscles and bug bites.
- **A staycation** – Cozy, affordable, and involves sleeping in your own bed. The ultimate lazy option.

Your choice depends on:

- **Who you are:** A sun-worshipper, a history buff, an adrenaline junkie, or just someone who wants a stress-free break.
- **What you want:** Total relaxation, new experiences, a food tour, or just to avoid arguing over itineraries.
- **Your challenges:** Agreeing on the same pace, staying within budget, or resisting the urge to check work emails.

The moment a destination doesn't match your travel style, you *know* it's not the one.

ASK AI RECOGNITION

Let's look at your brand. Based on your current website:

- Who is it for? Or is it for "everyone"?
- Are the aspirations and goals of the ideal customer clear?
- What are their challenges and problems?

Ask your favorite AI chat bot.

Get the prompt. Copy, paste, adapt and run.

Get the Prompt

WHY THIS MATTERS (A LOT)

Imagine your brand is a party. If people don't instantly get **who it's for, what the vibe is, and whether they'll enjoy themselves**, they're not stepping inside. They'll keep walking—maybe straight into your competitor's event where the snacks are better.

Recognition is that **snap decision** where someone decides:

"Yes! This is for me."

"Nope, moving on."

If your ideal customer **recognizes themselves** in your brand, they'll stay, explore, and engage. If they don't, they're gone before you can even say, "*Wait! We have exactly what you need!*"

Striking the Right Balance

For niche brands, this is easier—you can be hyper-specific. If you sell vegan hiking boots for left-handed adventurers, your audience either **immediately** sees themselves in your offer… or they don't.

But for broader brands, the challenge is **staying clear without being too narrow or too generic**.

- **Too specific?** You exclude potential customers who could love your offer.
- **Too broad?** You become forgettable—like a restaurant menu with 200 options, none of which sound great.

Check Yourself: Are You Getting Recognition Right?

Ask yourself these questions:

- **Who is your ideal customer?** If they landed on your page, would they say, *"This is exactly what I need!"*?
- **What do they want to accomplish?** Is it clear that *you* help them do that?
- **What are their challenges?** Do they instantly feel like you understand them?
- **Would they pick you over competitors?** Or are you blending into the crowd?

Final Takeaway:

You don't have time to convince people they belong—you have **seconds** to make them *feel* it. Make that first impression count.

FEATURES
DESIGN
PRICE
$99
REVIEWS

PERCEPTION 05

How are they different? What do I compare them to? Is their offer clear?

So, you've passed the first test—your customer thinks, "*Okay, this brand might be for me.*" But now, their brain shifts gears. It's no longer just a gut feeling; it's moves up to the brain.

- How are they different from the other options?
- Do I trust them?
- Is what they offer clear, or do I need a translator?

If your brand doesn't nail this moment, the customer **hesitates**—and hesitation is the enemy. Because when people are confused, overwhelmed, or skeptical, they do the easiest thing possible: *nothing.*

It's about understanding. Clarity is key.

Clarity is key.

STANDPOINT

The brands that stand out aren't just different—they **stand for something**. They take a clear **posture**, a defined **stance**, and a unique way of tackling their customers' challenges.

Think about it:

- **Patagonia** doesn't just sell outdoor gear—it fights for the planet.
- **LEGO** isn't just a toy company—it champions creativity, problem-solving, and learning through play.
- **Oatly** isn't just an oat milk brand—it's a rebellion against dairy, wrapped in playful, irreverent marketing.

Your **standpoint** isn't just about **what you do**—it's about **how you see the world** and **how you challenge the status quo**.

Ask Yourself:

- What do you **believe** about your industry that others don't?
- What are you **rejecting** that others blindly accept?
- How does your unique **approach** make life better for your customers?

Your standpoint isn't just a tagline—it's the **energy behind your brand**. Get it right, and you won't just attract customers—you'll create **believers**.

CATEGORY

We humans **love** to categorize things - it's how our brains make sense of the chaos. It's also why customers automatically **compare** your brand to something familiar.

- Are you "**just another marketing agency**" or the "**conversion-obsessed brand storytellers**"?
- Are you "**a budgeting app**" or the "**AI-powered financial coach in your pocket**"?
- Are you "**a running shoe**" or "**the only sneaker designed for people who actually hate running**"?

You don't always get to **choose** the category customers put you in—but you can **influence it**.

Ask Yourself:

- What are customers **already** comparing you to? (*And is it helping or hurting you?*)
- What **category shift** would make you stand out? (*Are you a "law firm" or a "legal fixer for startups"?*)
- Can you **create a new category** that makes you the only option? (*Think "plant-based meat" before it was a thing.*)

If you define your own category, you **own the narrative**—and when you own the narrative, you stop competing on price and start leading the conversation.

TRUST

Trust is the foundation of every purchase decision. But **trust isn't something you tell people to have—it's something you show**.

Think of it like **choosing a babysitter**. If you're leaving your kid with someone, you want proof they're reliable. Would you trust them just because they say, "*Don't worry, I'm great with kids!*"? **Nope**. But if they have glowing references, CPR certification, and a bunch of happy parents vouching for them, suddenly you're listening.

Your brand is no different. Customers won't just take your word for it—you need to prove it with:

- **Social proof** (reviews, testimonials, case studies)
- **Recognizable credibility** (big-name clients, media features, certifications)
- **Professionalism** (good design, clear messaging, no typos—because nothing says "trust us" like spelling mistakes)

If you don't build trust early, your customer's perception is, "*This looks sketchy.*" And sketchy doesn't sell.

VALUES – MORE THAN JUST A MARKETING GIMMICK

Customers today aren't just buying **products**—they're buying into **beliefs**. They want brands that align with their values, not just their wallets.

- **Beauty brands** now wear "cruelty-free" like a badge of honor—because animal testing is a dealbreaker for many.
- **Glasses and shoe companies** give back, offering a "buy one, donate one" model that turns purchases into purpose.
- **Restaurants** proudly source local, organic ingredients—not just for flavor, but to reassure customers they're making ethical choices.
- **Companies across industries** pledge to plant trees, cut plastic waste, or go carbon-neutral—because sustainability sells.

But here's the catch: **values aren't just slogans**. Customers can sniff out performative "greenwashing" or empty activism **a mile away**. If your brand claims to stand for something, it needs to **show it, live it, and back it up**—or risk losing trust.

Ask Yourself:

- What does your brand truly **believe in**—beyond profit?
- What **causes or ethics** matter most to your customers?
- How can you **demonstrate your values** in a way that feels authentic, not just trendy?

People don't just choose brands anymore—they **align** with them. Make sure your values aren't just written on your website but **woven into everything you do**.

OFFER

A confused customer doesn't become a customer.

If your brand can't explain its offer **clearly and simply**, people won't **ask for clarification—they'll just leave**.

Think about these two restaurant signs:

One makes you think, "*Wait... what?*"

The other makes you **hungry**.

If your brand message makes people stop and *figure it out*, you've already lost them.

BOTTOM LINE: PERCEPTION CAN MAKE OR BREAK YOU

Customers don't give brands extra chances. If they feel confused, uncertain, or unimpressed, they move on. Fast.

So, take a hard look at your brand and ask yourself:

- **What makes you different from competitors (and is it obvious)?**
- **Would a stranger instantly understand what you do?**
- **Does your messaging sound like a real person—or a corporate robot?**
- **Would you trust your own brand if you were a customer?**

If you hesitated on any of these, it's time to refine your perception. Because if customers aren't **clear** on why they should choose you, they won't.

ASK AI PERCEPTION

Back to your brand.

- How are you different?
- What is your standpoint? What category are you in?
- What do you do?
- Why should you be trusted?

Ask your favorite AI chat bot.

Get the prompt. Copy, paste, adapt and run.

Get the Prompt

PROJECTION 06

What will it be like? How will my life be better?

Change is hard. Doing nothing? *That's easy.*

Even when customers love what you're offering, their brain whispers:

- *"What if this is too complicated?"*
- *"What if I don't have time to figure this out?"*
- *"What if I regret it and feel stupid?"*

Before people buy, they **mentally test-drive the experience**. They picture what it will be like **after** they commit. If they can't see a clear, positive future, they hesitate. And hesitation kills conversions.

Your job? **Make that future crystal clear**. Remove the uncertainty, paint the best-case scenario, and make them feel confident that saying *yes* is the easiest decision they'll make today.

EXPERIENCE

Think about the last time you almost bought something but didn't.

- Maybe it was a **fitness program**—but you imagined struggling through workouts and quitting in a week.
- Maybe it was a **software subscription**—but you dreaded learning yet another tool.
- Maybe it was a **consulting service**—but you weren't sure if it would actually solve your problem.

Your customers feel the same way. They don't just ask, "*Do I want this?*" They ask, "*What will this actually be like?*"

So, **paint the picture for them**. Will they get fast, seamless onboarding? Will they feel an immediate impact? Will the experience be easy, enjoyable—even fun?

If they can see it, they'll believe it.

STAKES

In "Recognition", you declare your main claim: help with an aspiration and a challenge. Of course, your offer solves many problems.

Your customer is at the tipping point—one tiny push, and they'll either say **yes** or walk away.

This is where you **raise the stakes**. If they hesitate, **what's the cost?**

- **A business owner** who doesn't invest in the right tools keeps wasting hours on inefficient systems.
- **A professional** who doesn't upskill stays stuck in the same position for years.
- **A customer** who doesn't switch to your service keeps dealing with frustration and poor results.

Remind them: **doing nothing isn't neutral—it has a price, too.**

If they walk away, they're choosing to stay exactly where they are. If they say **yes**, they're choosing a better future.

POSITIVE FUTURE

Let Them See Themselves Winning

Once hesitation is gone, it's time to **spark excitement**.

Your customer isn't just buying a product or service - they're stepping into a **better version of their life**. They need to **see it, feel it, believe it**.

- **A new entrepreneur** envisions themselves confidently pitching their business, customers lining up to buy.
- **A team using your software** imagines work flowing effortlessly, projects getting done without stress.
- **A traveler booking a trip** sees themselves sipping coffee on a sunlit terrace, no itinerary - just pure freedom.

This isn't about explaining features or logic—it's about creating a **mental movie** where they are the main character, thriving.

How Do You Help Them See It?

- **Use sensory details** – Can they picture the moment? The feeling? The ease?
- **Make it immediate** – What's the first sign they made the right choice?
- **Turn it into an experience** – What does success **look** like with you?

The future isn't just better—it's **real**. And now, it's **within reach**.

BOTTOM LINE: REMOVE DOUBT, BUILD DESIRE

Customers won't move forward if they're unsure about what happens next.

Take a moment to step into their shoes:

- Can they instantly picture what working with you feels like?
- Do they feel reassured that it's easy, smooth, and worth it?
- Have you made the stakes clear—both the risk of inaction and the reward of saying yes?

People don't buy products. **They buy better futures**. Make that future irresistible.

ASK AI PROJECTION

Your brand again.

- What is the experience with your company like?
- What are some examples of challenges or problems that it addresses?
- What positive future does it promise? Do you come away imagining how your life would be better?
- Is the next step clear?

Ask your favorite AI chat bot.

Get the prompt. Copy, paste, adapt and run.

Get the Prompt

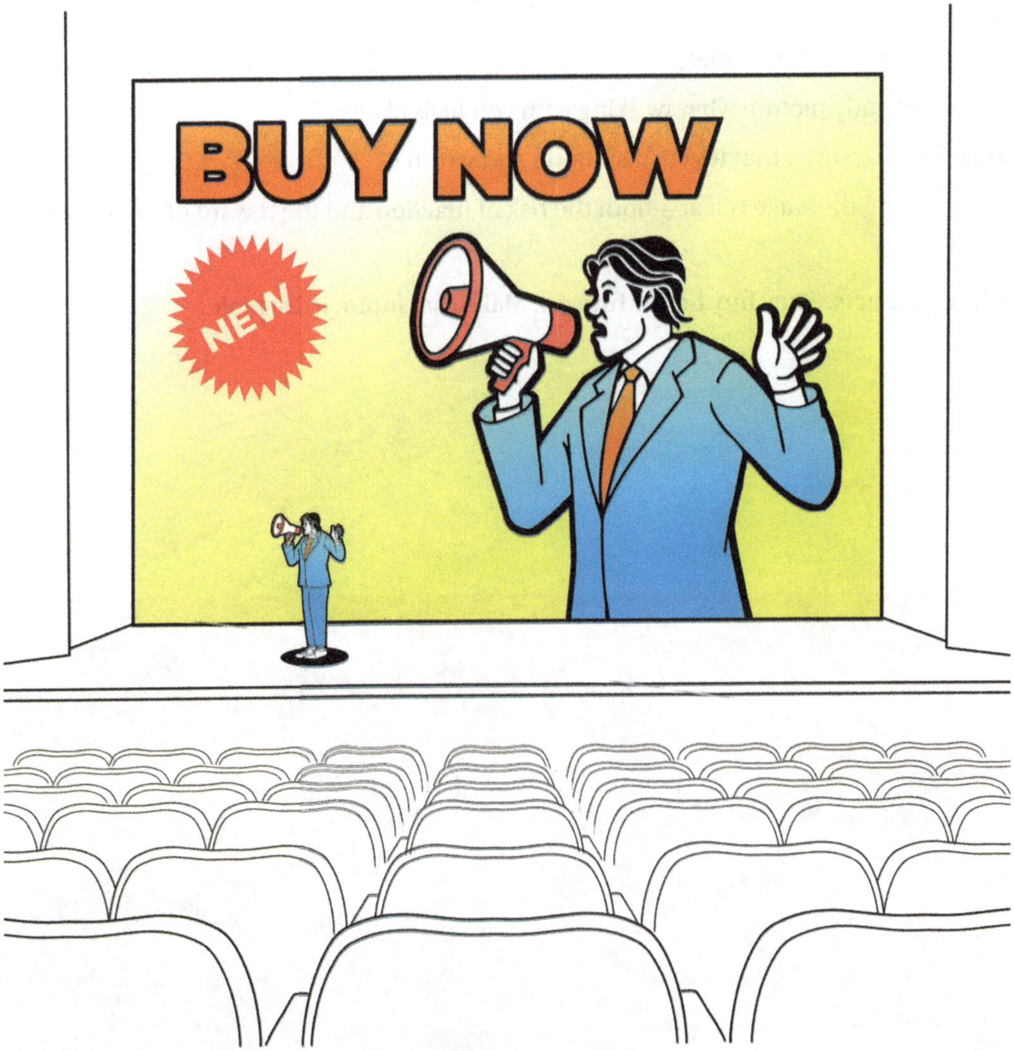
BUY NOW
NEW

SELF-CENTERED BRANDS 07

What happens when brands don't take their customers' standpoint, and only talk about themselves, about what they do?

When brands focus more on themselves than their customers, they create disconnects that can alienate their audience at every stage of the engagement journey. Let's explore two examples —one B2C and one B2B—and see how they fail at each step of Recognition, Perception, and Projection. And yes, brace yourself—this is going to be like watching a slowmotion train wreck.

EXAMPLES

The B2C Gardening Service

Recognition

Imagine a homeowner, Maria, looking for a gardening service to maintain her backyard. She searches online and comes across "GreenPro Landscaping," a company whose website prominently displays awards, certifications, and technical jargon about soil types and advanced irrigation techniques.

Maria's immediate reaction is: "***Is this for me?***"

Unfortunately, GreenPro Landscaping's homepage fails to answer that question. Instead of lush garden photos or happy homeowners, it looks more like a LinkedIn profile for a very proud agronomist. Maria quickly feels overwhelmed and unsure if they cater to residential clients like her or focus on large commercial projects. She bounces faster than a squirrel spotting a bird feeder.

Perception

Out of malicious curiosity, Maria revisits the site and decides to dig deeper. As she browses their services, she encounters long, dense descriptions about their methods: "*Our soil aeration process integrates advanced techniques such as core drilling to enhance root penetration and nitrogen absorption.*" While the information might impress an agronomist, Maria is left confused and frustrated. "*Why are they talking about nitrogen absorption? I just want my yard to look pretty,*" she thinks.

By failing to clarify the value of their services in a relatable way, GreenPro Landscaping alienates Maria. Instead of showing her how they can simplify her life and beautify her outdoor space, they bog her down with irrelevant technicalities. At this point, Maria's gardening dreams are wilting.

Projection

Maria wonders what it would be like to hire GreenPro. She's unable to find any detailed testimonials, before-and-after photos, or clear explanations of the process. Instead of envisioning a hassle-free experience and a transformed backyard, she imagines confusing consultations filled with jargon and unexpected costs. It's like picturing a blind date where the person won't stop talking about their PhD thesis on soil acidity.

Ultimately, Maria hires a competitor whose website simply says: "*We create beautiful gardens for busy homeowners. Leave the work to us and enjoy your outdoor space.*"

How This Hurts GreenPro Landscaping

By being self-centered, GreenPro loses customers like Maria who seek clarity, empathy, and reassurance. Their expertise may be top-notch, but their failure to position it in terms of customer value makes their messaging ineffective. They're not just losing individual customers—they're losing trust, word-of-mouth recommendations, and long-term growth opportunities. Green thumbs don't grow on self-centered soil.

The B2B Fleet Management Service

Recognition

George is the operations manager for a mid-sized logistics company, tasked with finding a fleet management service to optimize vehicle management and reduce costs. He comes across "Fleet first Solutions," whose website leads with statements like: "*Founded in 1998, FleetFirst Solutions is the industry leader in telematics.*" The rest of the page lists their awards, the size of their team, and the number of clients they've served.

George's immediate reaction is skepticism. "*Okay, they're big and experienced, but do they understand my business?*" FleetFirst fails to acknowledge its potential customers - small and medium-sized businesses like George's - and instead focuses on boasting about its scale and longevity. George isn't sure if they're the right fit for his specific needs. It's like a restaurant bragging about their Michelin stars without mentioning what kind of food they serve.

Perception

Despite his initial doubts, George schedules a demo with FleetFirst. During the presentation, the salesperson spends most of the time highlighting the platform's complex features, like detailed diagnostics and custom integrations. While these might be impressive to a tech-savvy audience, George is left wondering: "*How will this actually help me save money or improve efficiency?*"

The sales rep never takes the time to ask George about his company's unique challenges, such as fuel costs and driver accountability. Instead, the pitch feels like a one-size-fits-all monologue, making George question whether FleetFirst even understands the needs of smaller fleets. It's like trying to sell a sports car to someone who's looking for a reliable minivan.

Projection

George tries to imagine working with FleetFirst but struggles to picture a smooth implementation. Their materials are filled with buzzwords like "*AI-powered analytics*" and "*scalable solutions*," but there's no concrete information about how long setup takes, what kind of support is available, or how the system integrates with existing tools. He worries about high upfront costs, endless training sessions, and minimal ROI.

In contrast, a competitor's pitch includes a clear implementation timeline, straightforward pricing, and case studies showcasing real-world savings. George chooses the competitor, leaving FleetFirst with another missed opportunity. FleetFirst's pitch may as well have come with a "For Tech Nerds Only" disclaimer.

How This Hurts FleetFirst Solutions

FleetFirst's self-centered approach—focusing on their accolades and features rather than customer outcomes - costs them potential clients like George. Their failure to understand and address their audience's pain points leads to lost sales, negative perceptions, and wasted marketing efforts. Over time, this approach damages their reputation and stunts their growth in competitive markets. The wheels of their business grind to a halt, ironically enough.

KEY TAKEAWAYS

In both examples, the companies failed because they centered their messaging around themselves rather than their customers. Whether it's a homeowner seeking a beautiful backyard or an operations manager looking for efficiency, people need to feel seen, understood, and reassured.

Recognition, Perception, and Projection are opportunities to build trust and connection - but only if the focus is on the customer. Brands that embrace a customer-centered approach can transform these stages into powerful moments of engagement, creating long-term loyalty and success. Self-centered brands? They're destined to remain the butt of marketing jokes - and not in a good way.

WHAT'S NEXT?

That was a lot - take a breath.

Now that we understand how customers **recognize, perceive, and project themselves** into a brand, it's time to go deeper.

Next, we'll flip perspectives and step into **their world**—what they want, what drives them, and what truly makes them tick.

Then, we'll turn the spotlight back on your brand, reassessing your **offer, positioning, and messaging** to make sure everything aligns.

Only then can we craft a story that doesn't just get their attention—but **pulls them in and makes them care.**

Let's get to it.

PART 3: UNDERSTANDING

To tell a story that sticks, you need to see the world through the eyes of your customer (or investor, or boss). What do they want? What do they feel? Then, flip the lens on your own brand—because sometimes, the outside view is way more revealing than the inside one. Time to sharpen your focus!

standpoint
standpoint

PRACTICAL TIPS 08

Team of customer facing people. White board and sticky notes.

This isn't a book to read and forget - it's a book to **use**. You'll get the most value out of it if you actively engage with the method. So, before diving in, let's set the stage.

The Power of Collective Thinking

Great ideas don't emerge in a vacuum. They come from **conversation, collaboration, and iteration**. That's why the best way to go through this process is **with a team** - especially people who interact with customers. They have insights that are gold.

Imagine a room with a whiteboard, sticky notes in every color, and a group of people who actually know what your customers care about. That's the dream scenario. If that's not possible, grab a notebook, open a doc, or fire up a collaboration tool - just make sure you're **writing things down**. Ideas disappear faster than you think.

The Process: Hands-on, Messy, but Worth It

For each canvas, each section, each question—**throw ideas on the table**. No filtering, no overthinking. Build on each other's thoughts. The goal is to **see beyond the obvious**, to **challenge assumptions**, and to **spot patterns**.

Use **one idea per sticky note** (physical or digital). Different colors? Even better. It helps visualize patterns. But don't get too caught up in the aesthetics—clarity over beauty.

In Real Life

- **Print the canvases big.** Bigger than you think. Tape them on a wall.
- **Sticky notes are your best friend.** The more, the better.
- **Write BIG and CLEAR.** If people need to squint, you're doing it wrong. No ballpoint pens—use markers.

Online

- Use a **digital whiteboard tool** (Miro, Mural, FigJam, Notion—pick your favorite).
- **Upload the canvases** and create sticky notes digitally.
- **Encourage participation**. Silence isn't golden here—it's wasted potential.

AI Assistance

Your AI assistant isn't just a chatbot—it's a **sparring partner**. Use it to:

- **Brainstorm** ("What are possible aspirations and challenges of [target customer]?")
- **Clarify thinking** ("Explain this in simpler terms.")
- **Challenge assumptions** ("What's a common misconception about this industry?")

You can **feed it your rough notes** and have it refine, summarize, or even point out what's missing. Think of it as an intern who works at lightning speed and never complains.

The Goal

By the end of this process, you won't just **understand** your brand's story—you'll have **built** it. So, grab your team (or your best thinking cap), and let's get started.

Practical Tips

Disclaimer

The examples are simplified versions to facilitate the understanding of the Storybuilding method. In real life, it's a lot messier.

In real life, it's a lot messier.

It could look like this.

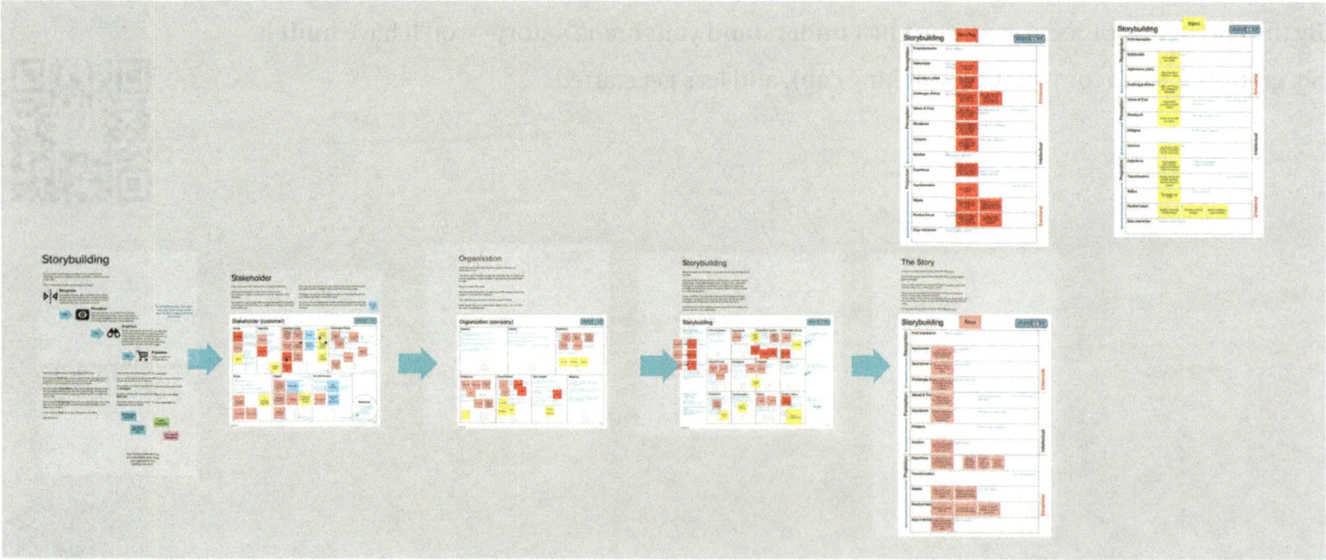

Or even like this.

YOUR
BRAND

YOUR STAKEHOLDERS (CUSTOMERS)

09

Who are your customers, and what are their aspirations and their challenges?

It's time to step into your customers' shoes. Literally. Lace them up, take a walk, and see the world from their perspective.

Forget—just for a moment—that you have an amazing product, that you're trying to sell something, or that your business is the answer to their problems. None of that matters unless you truly understand what's going on in their world first.

This is where most businesses get it wrong. They think, "*Our product is great, people should just get it.*" But customers don't care about your product. They care about what they want, what's standing in their way, and whether you can actually help them.

Think of this as method acting for business—you need to become your customer. What keeps them up at night? What makes them smile? What problems do they face that they haven't even realized are solvable?

Rethinking competition

Here's something that might challenge your thinking: your real competitors aren't always who you think they are. A movie theater's competition isn't just other theaters—it's Netflix, restaurants, walks in the park, or simply staying home with a good book. Anything that solves the same fundamental need is competition.

> *Anything that solves the same fundamental need is competition.*

This broader view of competition helps you understand the real choices your customers face. They're not just choosing between different versions of your product—they're choosing between different ways to solve their problems or achieve their goals.

So, let's roll up our sleeves and really get into your customers' heads. We'll explore their dreams, feel their frustrations, and discover those perfect moments when they're most ready to hear about your solution. Just remember—this isn't about you anymore. It's all about them.

And here's the beautiful part: when you truly understand your customers, marketing stops feeling like pushing products and starts feeling like helping friends solve their problems. Which, let's be honest, is a much more enjoyable way to do business.

The Power of Customer Research

Of course, you can (and should) do proper market research and customer interviews. Ask your existing customers why they chose you—their answers might surprise you. One company I worked with thought their customers loved their advanced features, only to discover that most customers chose them because their customer service team was exceptionally friendly. Advanced tech? Nice to have. Warm, helpful humans? Game-changer.

These insights are pure gold. They help you understand not just what customers say they want, but what they actually value. Sometimes these aren't the same thing—just like how people might say they want a healthy salad but end up ordering pizza. Understanding this gap between stated preferences and actual behavior can be the key to creating compelling marketing messages.

So, let's dive in.

We will be using the "Stakeholder (Customer)" canvas. (P. 80)

Stakeholder (Customer) Canvas

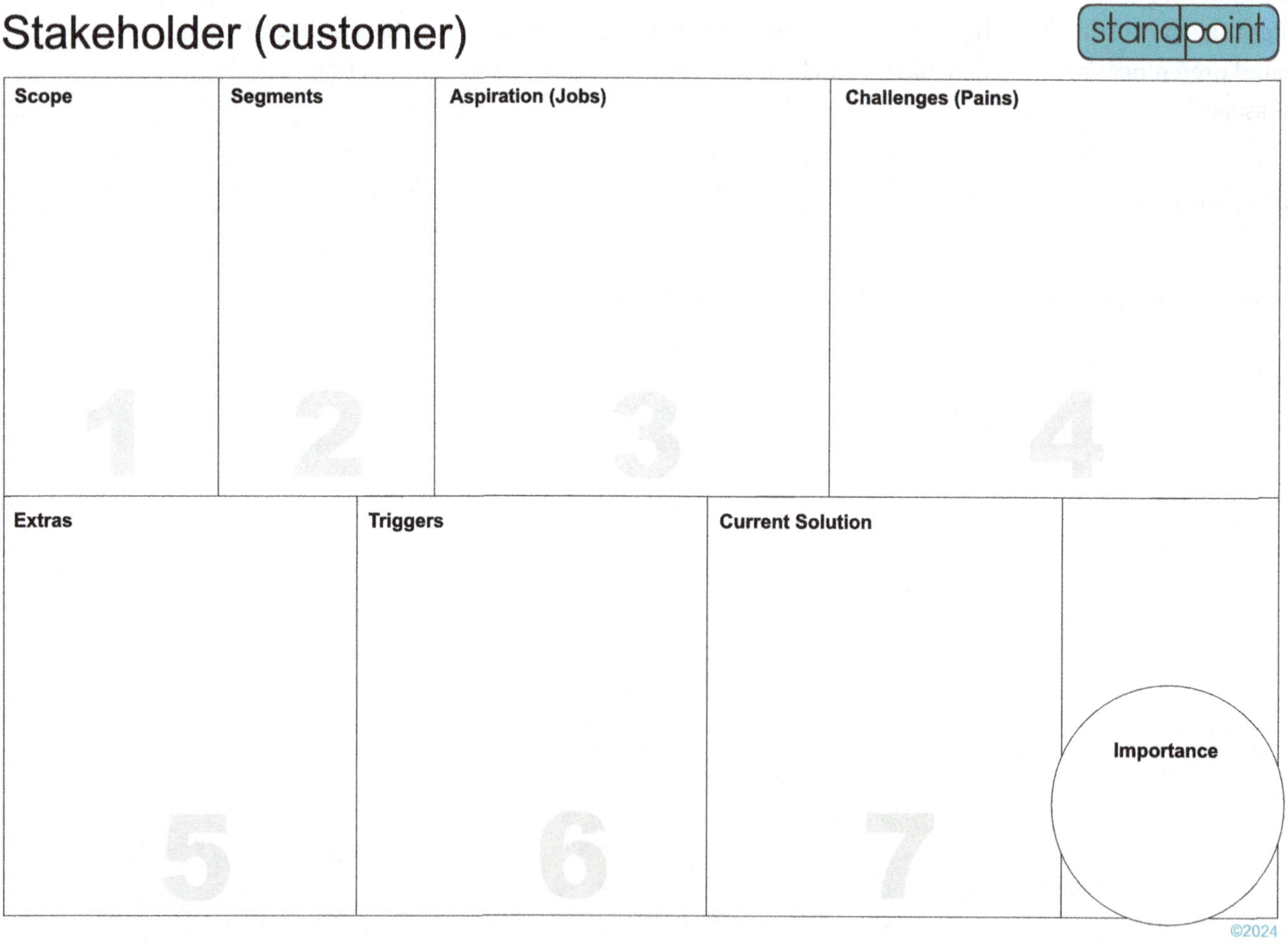

THE CONTEXT

First, you need to define the context: the scope of the offer and the customer segments you want to address.

1. Scope

Here's a common trap: trying to understand your customer's entire life story when you only need to know about the part that intersects with your solution. It's like a dentist trying to understand your workout routine—interesting, perhaps, but not relevant to your cavity.

The trick is finding the sweet spot—not too narrow ("people who need a blue widget on Thursdays") and not too broad ("anyone who breathes oxygen"). You want to understand enough context to be relevant and helpful, but not so much that you lose focus on what matters for your specific offering.

Take the general scope of your offer, the category as seen from the customer's standpoint.

Define the scope based on the general goal or problem to be solved. Not too narrow, being exactly or very close to what you offer. Not too broad, encompassing things that are not relevant.

For example:

- Mattress or Sleep
- To do apps or Organization
- Selling your company
- Increasing cybersecurity
- Hungry

The scope is how your customer thinks.

2. Segments

Before we can understand what your customers want, we need to figure out *who* they are. And no, "everyone" is not an acceptable answer.

Who is your customer, audience, or important stakeholder?

We want to understand what truly drives different groups of customers—their aspirations, challenges, and those "aha!" moments when they realize they need what you offer.

Are there defining characteristics?

How can they be grouped? By aspiration, by problem, by industry, by role, by risk-tolerance?

Segmentation strategy is beyond the scope of this book. But remember a few important points.

Segmentation is expensive. Another segment means another message, another marketing strategy, other assets, other sales scripts, ... So, choose wisely.

Segmentation isn't demographics, or not most importantly. Segment by how they formulate their aspirations and challenges in their mind.

If two very different people have the same goal and problem, they aren't different segments. A young professional and a retired grandparent might both buy the same noise-canceling headphones. One wants them for productivity in a loud co-working space; the other wants them to tune out their grandkids watching cartoons at full volume. They both want to concentrate in a noisy environment. Are they really different segments?

Sometimes the same actual person can be part of two segments. Think of a young adult who buys a pair of Nike shoes for running and another to look cool. Athletic segment or lifestyle segment? Both!

Remember that we want your customer to recognize themselves. Segments can be internal identities (e.g. athlete vs jogger).

You can use a separate canvas for each segment, but it can be easier to put them all on the same one, using different color sticky notes for the different segments. You can highlight similarities and differences.

YOUR CUSTOMER'S MIND

Now get into your customer's mind.

Think of your customer's mind as a complex landscape—not unlike a city with different neighborhoods, each representing different needs and desires. To navigate this landscape effectively, we'll use four key concepts: Aspirations, Challenges, Extras, and Triggers.

Interestingly, you'll find these concepts often overlap, like a Venn diagram of human motivation. For instance, "finding more customers" could be framed as an aspiration ("*We want to grow our business!*") or as a challenge (*"We're frustrated by our inability to attract new clients*"). The goal isn't to perfectly categorize these elements—it's to understand how your customers see them.

Aspiration	**Challenge**
Grow business	Not finding clients
Increase loyalty	Reducing churn
Increase margins	Lowering expenses
Advance one's career	Stop getting passed over for a promotion
Save time	Stop wasting time
Increase quality	Reduce defects
Hire great talent	Can't find required skills

Don't stress it. The point is to get out the ideas, not necessarily to put them perfectly in the right spot.

3. Aspiration (Jobs)

Customers don't wake up thinking, *"I need a product."* They wake up thinking, *"I need to achieve my goal or solve my problem."*

So, let's figure out what they're trying to accomplish.

Every customer decision is driven by a mix of rational and emotional needs. To craft stories that resonate, you must address both.

> ***Every customer decision is driven by a mix of rational and emotional needs.***

Rational needs are practical and problem-solving. They focus on measurable outcomes like saving time, reducing costs, or improving efficiency. For example:

- A parent looks for a car seat with top-rated safety features.
- A freelancer needs a to-do app to manage multiple projects.
- A person suffering from stress wants to track their sleep

Emotional needs tap into desires like belonging, recognition, or security. They reflect aspirations and feelings, often driving the "why" behind decisions. For instance:

- The parent wants to feel like a responsible caregiver.
- The freelancer seeks confidence and a sense of achievement.
- The person suffering from stress wants to wake up refreshed, energized, and in control of their health.

3 levels

Think of aspirations as your customers' North Star—what they're moving toward. Write down the obvious goals of your client.

But don't stop there.

Here's where it gets interesting: these aspirations often exist on multiple levels, like Russian nesting dolls.

Starting with a specific goal that you identified, can you imagine a "higher up" aspiration? In the same way, can you imagine a more practical task that they need to get done?

You can think of it in a similar way as the five whys exercise, where you keep asking why until you understand the problem fully.

From the goal "a hook in my wall", you could be more aspirational with "hang a painting" or even "make their house feel more like a home", or more practical with "drill a hole" or "buy a drill bit".

This multi-level understanding is crucial because different customers might connect with different levels of the same aspiration. Some might respond to practical messaging about hole-drilling efficiency, while others might be moved by emotional appeals about creating their dream home.

Often, we know what our product does, so we think we know what our customer wants to accomplish. But that's not always what's happening in their head. So go broader, go higher, go lower, and explore what your customer could possibly want to accomplish.

The customer of a marketing agency could be looking to create a campaign, create a marketing strategy, boost their sales, or grow their business.

The customer of home security alarm system could be looking just for an alarm system, for protecting their house, or for feeling secure.

The customer of an enterprise fleet management system could be looking to lower costs, to be more efficient, to be the hero of their company.

The customer of a corporate wellness coaching company could be looking to improve employee morale, to improve productivity, to be seen as a good company, to be successful.

You can sort the aspirations you have identified from "practical" to "aspirational".

Try to imagine how your customer sees their aspiration.

ASK AI ASPIRATIONS

As your ideal customer:

- What do you want to accomplish?
- What are your motivations?
- What emotions are linked to this?

Ask your favorite AI chat bot.

Get the Prompt ◀ ***Get the prompt.*** Copy, paste, adapt and run.

4. Challenges (Pains)

Now that we know what they want, let's talk about what's stopping them.

What is holding them back?

What are the obstacles, problems, pains, and annoyances that keep them from attaining their goals?

What are the negative emotions that accompany them, such as frustration, anger, or fear?

How aware are they of the things that hinder their progress?

Is there a major societal, technical, or economic change (e.g., AI) that could be a threat?

In the same way, brainstorm not only the different challenges, but also the different ways the customer can perceive their challenges.

> ***Brainstorm not only the different challenges, but also the different ways the customer can perceive their challenges.***

Imagine selling an app that helps freelancers track invoices. Your customer isn't just looking for "invoice software." They want to stop chasing clients for payments. They want cash flow without awkward emails. They want *peace of mind.* That's what you're really selling.

One person's dream can be another's frustration.

"I want to run a marathon to challenge myself" is an aspiration.

"I can't even run a mile without gasping for air" is a challenge.

Same end goal—running—but whether it feels exciting or overwhelming depends on where they're starting from. And often, the solution is the same: a solid training plan.

It is important to take your customer's standpoint, and to understand how they see the issue. You might put the same sticky note in both squares.

Challenges are the villains in your customer's story—the obstacles standing between them and their goals. But here's a fascinating twist: not all challenges are created equal in your customer's mind.

Some challenges are like a blaring car alarm—impossible to ignore and actively seeking a solution. Others are more like background noise—problems your customers have learned to live with, perhaps not even recognizing them as solvable issues.

Take parking in a busy city. Many people have simply accepted the daily struggle of finding a spot as "just the way things are." If you're selling a smart parking solution, part of your job might be helping people realize this daily frustration isn't actually necessary.

So, you can classify the challenges you come up with on a range between those that are obvious to your customers, to those where they are still unaware that there is a problem that is solvable.

It is also important to identify the emotions that are linked to the challenges. People can be frustrated, angry, scared, upset… identifying these emotions will help craft the story in a way that mirrors them.

Your job? Not just to solve problems, but to show customers *why* those problems matter and how life can be better on the other side.

Pro tip: If a customer doesn't *feel* their problem deeply, they won't be motivated to solve it. Your messaging should amplify their frustration just enough that they *want* to take action.

ASK AI CHALLENGES

Take the standpoint of your customer:

- What are the challenges you hope to address?
- What are your frustrations, anger or fears?
- What is keeping you from accomplishing your goals?
- What emotions are linked to this?

Ask your favorite AI chat bot.

Get the prompt. Copy, paste, adapt and run.

Get the Prompt

5. Extras

Aspirations and challenges? Super important. But let's be real—they're not the *only* things driving a decision. The broader experience matters just as much, sometimes even more.

That's where the "Extras" come in—the emotional and experiential factors that influence choices in ways customers might not even consciously realize.

Think about a to-do list app. At its core, it's just a glorified checklist, right? But why do some people obsess over a sleek, minimalist interface while others want color-coded categories and confetti animations when they complete a task? Because people don't just want to *be* organized— they want to *feel* organized. They want an experience that reflects the control, clarity, and calm they crave in their daily lives.

So, ask yourself:

- What are their values?
- How do they want to feel?
- How do they want to be perceived?
- What kind of experience are they really looking for?

The Movie Theater Mystery

Ever noticed that in some theaters, particularly in the back row, every other armrest mysteriously disappears? Instead of individual seats, there are cozy little sofas for two. Coincidence? Not a chance.

When you think about a theater's audience segments, couples are a big one. And let's be honest— they're not just there for the Dolby Surround Sound. Watching a movie together is about more than just the film. It's about the experience—the dim lights, the quiet intimacy, and yes, the chance to hold hands without awkwardly battling a plastic armrest.

Smart businesses understand these unspoken desires and design their offerings accordingly.

Designing for Experience

Beyond solving a problem, what kind of emotional experience are your customers looking for? What's their mindset when engaging with your product or service?

These insights don't just add depth to your brand's story—they can also spark ideas for small, lowcost enhancements that make a big impact. Sometimes, the tiniest tweaks can transform a standard offering into something that feels tailor-made.

So, step back and think about your customers' emotions, sensations, and perceptions. Because sometimes, the difference between a good product and a *great* one isn't in what it does—it's in how it makes people *feel.*

6. Triggers

Timing, as they say, is everything. Triggers are those magical moments when your offering suddenly becomes incredibly relevant to your customer's life. Think of them as windows of opportunity—moments when your message is most likely to resonate.

For instance, a home insurance company could send mailers to everyone in town. Or they could focus on new homeowners, recent parents, or people who've just experienced a minor household incident. The same message hits differently when it arrives at the right moment.

What triggers the need for a solution?
What situation, event, or emotion brings the scope of your offer to the front of your mind?

What situation, event, or emotion brings the scope of your offer to the front of your mind?

What trigger moments are specific to your offer? What situations make what you're selling more interesting to the person concerned?

The beauty of understanding triggers is that it often leads to practical marketing strategies. Some triggers, like new business registrations or home purchases, come with publicly available lists. Others might be more subtle, requiring you to create content that helps customers recognize themselves in specific situations.

Many of those situations are clear in the customer's mind, but can't be directly found out. Accordingly, you can advertise or post stories about those moments on social media. The customers that are in those situations will recognize themselves. For example, if you create an advertisement talking about the risks linked to serious health issues, and the interesting options for insurance to protect you from those risks, the people that are in that situation will recognize themselves, and you will grab their interest.

Trigger Moments:

- A startup just got funding and *now* needs a branding agency.
- A homeowner just had a pipe burst and *now* needs a plumber.
- A marketer just got a terrible engagement report and *now* needs a new strategy.

Your job: Find these moments and be there when they happen.

Example: A gym running ads *right after* New Year's = smart. A moving company targeting people *before* their lease ends = even smarter.

Can you identify trigger moments linked to your offer?

Can you make a list of customers who are in those trigger moments (knowable)?

Would customers who are in those trigger moments recognize themselves if you describe a trigger moment (recognizable)?

ASK AI TRIGGERS

Your ideal client:

- What situation, event, or emotion triggers your need and brings the scope of this offer to the front of your mind?

Ask your favorite AI chat bot.

Get the Prompt

Get the prompt. Copy, paste, adapt and run.

7. Current situation

How are your customers managing their problem today?

Are they happy with their current approach, or just tolerating it?

Are they actively searching for something better, or have they simply given up?

There's *always* a current solution—whether it's a manual workaround, an outdated system, or simply ignoring the problem altogether. The "solution" to boredom might be skiing… or just binge-watching Netflix.

If your customer is frustrated and *actively* looking for a better option, selling to them is easier—they're already motivated. But if they've resigned themselves to their situation, believing their problem is just "how things are," you've got an extra challenge: before selling your solution, you first need to convince them that change is possible.

Look for two key opportunities:

1. **People deeply unhappy with their current situation**—they're primed for a switch.
2. **Flawed "solutions" that create more problems than they solve**—users will be open to a better alternative if they see the value.

Your job isn't just to offer a better way—it's to help them realize they *deserve* one.

Importance

By now, you've gathered a wealth of insights about your customer or stakeholder. Now comes the crucial step—sorting through it all to identify what truly matters.

Take a first pass and mark the most important elements from your customer's perspective. Think of it like starring key emails—some messages are interesting, but only a few really demand attention.

This step is essential. Hopefully, you've come up with a variety of ideas, but not all are equally impactful. Now's the time to narrow them down to the most promising ones.

Later, during the Storybuilding phase, you'll need three levels of importance:

1. **Core Drivers** – The *one or two* biggest aspirations and challenges that shape the story.
2. **Supporting Insights** – *Five to six* additional factors that add depth and reinforce the message.
3. **The Rest** – Useful, but not essential right now. Set them aside for later.

This process isn't about discarding ideas—it's about focusing on what will make the biggest impact.

REFLECTION

Go back to the first square: **Scope**. How did you define it? Now that you've stepped into your customer's world, does it still feel right? Or should it be expressed differently to better reflect *their* perspective?

Next, review your list of target segments. Does it feel too broad? If you've identified too many segments, see if you can consolidate some—fewer, well-defined segments are far more effective than a scattered approach. On the other hand, did you overlook any key groups? If so, revisit your canvas and refine your focus.

Now, go through each section again. Challenge yourself to think beyond the obvious—move from surface-level frustrations to deeper, more existential motivations. Stay within the scope of your offer, but forget the specifics of *what* you do. Your customers aren't thinking about your product or service—they're thinking about how it fits into their life and solves their problem.

Everything on this sheet is from *their* standpoint. Make sure it reflects *their* world, *their* challenges, and *their* aspirations—not just your assumptions.

The insights you've gathered here aren't just research; they're the backbone of our brand story.

Nail this, and your message won't just be heard—it'll *resonate.*

ACKNOWLEDGMENT

VPC inspiration ◀

Before developing my own canvases, my go to framework was the **Value Proposition Design canvas** by Alex Osterwalder and Yves Pigneur. The "Stakeholder (customer)" canvas is similar to the right side. Check out how I was inspired.

EXAMPLES

Part 5—starting on P. 209—is jam packed of full examples of the four steps of Storybuilding. Here are three examples of the Stakeholder canvas to give you an idea.

B2C: Indoor Gardening Kit For Small Spaces (P. 236)

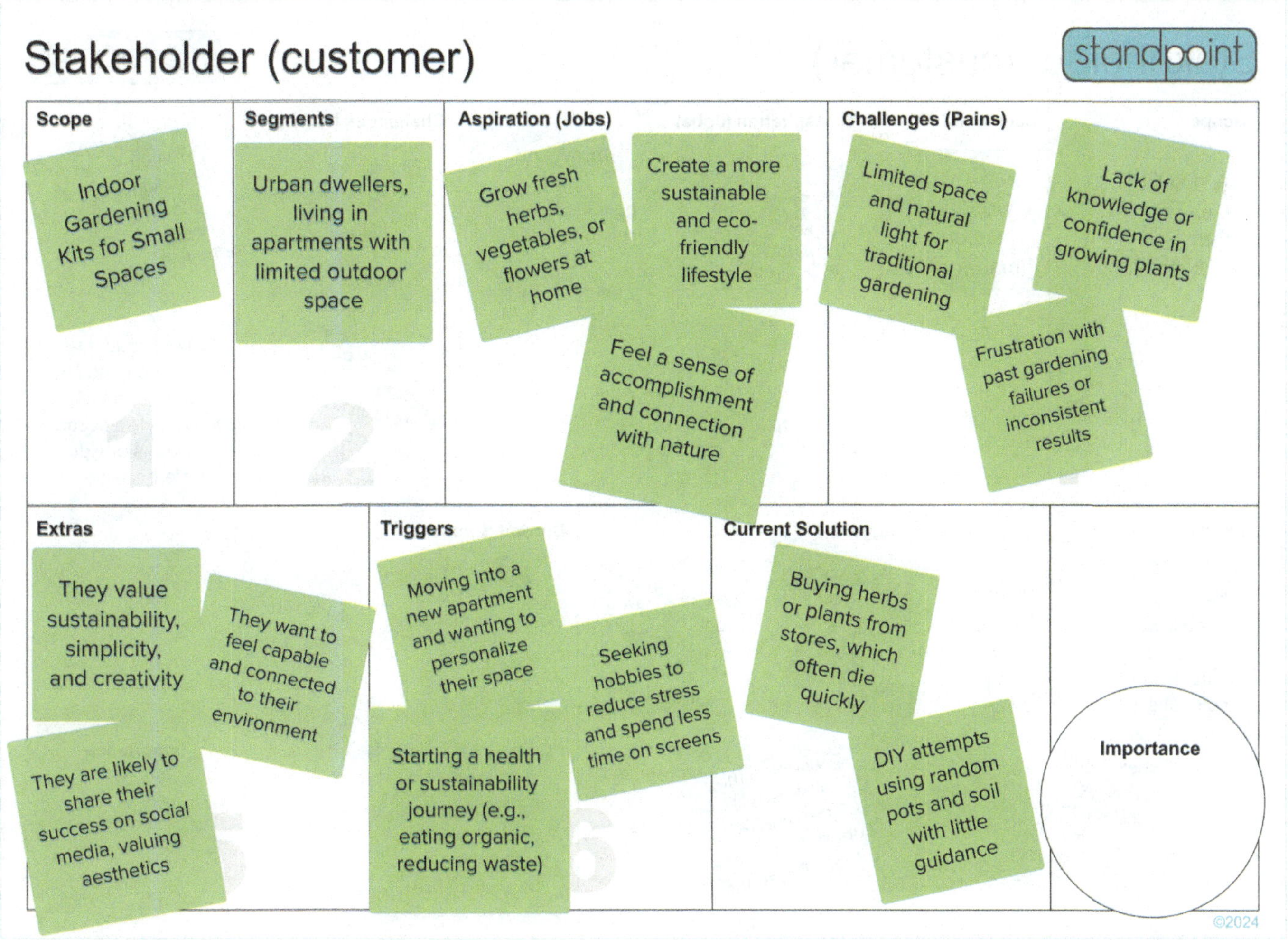

B2B: IT Support For Co-Working Spaces (P. 246)

Stakeholder (customer)

standpoint

Scope

- IT Support for Co-Working Spaces

Segments

- Co-working space managers

Aspiration (Jobs)

- Ensure seamless tech operations for tenants
- Attract and retain businesses with reliable, cutting-edge infrastructure
- Build a reputation as a tech-forward and hassle-free work environment

Challenges (Pains)

- Frequent Wi-Fi outages or slow internet speeds
- Tenant complaints about IT infrastructure or tech support
- Lack of expertise or resources to manage complex tech issues
- Struggling to meet tenant demands for advanced tech features like secure networks or video conferencing tools

Extras

- They value reliability, responsiveness, and future-proof solutions
- They want to feel confident that tech won't disrupt daily operations
- They prioritize tenant satisfaction and want to feel like problem-solvers

Triggers

- Experiencing repeated tenant complaints about connectivity issues
- Losing tenants to competitors with better tech infrastructure
- Expanding their space and needing to upgrade or scale their IT systems

Current Solution

- Patchwork solutions (e.g., hiring freelancers for tech support)
- Relying on generic internet providers without tailored service
- DIY troubleshooting that results in wasted time and temporary fixes

Importance

©2024

Handmade Art & Craft Marketplace (P. 262)

Stakeholder (customer) Sellers Buyers

standpoint

Scope

Handmade Art & Craft Marketplace

Segments

- Sellers (Independent Craftspersons)
- Buyers (Art Enthusiasts and Ethical Shoppers)

Aspiration (Jobs)

- Gain visibility and grow their personal brand
- Own unique, meaningful products with a story behind them
- Monetize their passion sustainably
- Support independent creators and eco-friendly practices
- Connect with a niche audience that values craftsmanship

Challenges (Pains)

- Lack of marketing and technical skills
- Finding authentic handmade items in a market flooded with replicas
- Difficulty managing payments and logistics
- Limited trust in unknown online sellers
- Competing with mass-produced goods
- Lack of knowledge about artisans' backgrounds or production methods

Extras

- Value authenticity, creativity, and fair trade
- Value uniqueness, transparency, and sustainability
- Want to feel empowered and appreciated for their work
- Want to feel connected to the products they buy and their creators

Triggers

- Completing a new collection or a unique piece
- Gift-giving occasions
- Receiving positive feedback from local buyers and wanting to expand
- Redecorating homes or celebrating personal milestones

Current Solution

- Selling at local markets or small retail shops with limited reach.
- Shopping at chain stores
- Social media selling with inconsistent results
- Shopping at large, impersonal online platforms

Importance

©2024

SIDE QUEST: TRIGGER MARKETING

A

WHY TIMING MATTERS MORE THAN EVER

Marketing isn't just about what you say—it's about when you say it. The best marketing doesn't feel like marketing at all; it feels like *timely* help. That's what **trigger marketing** is all about: identifying key moments in your customer's life when your offer becomes *incredibly relevant*—and being there when it counts.

A home insurance company could send flyers to every homeowner, but what if they only targeted new homeowners? A moving company could market to everyone, or just those whose leases are ending soon. Right place, right time = better results.

So how do you find these magic moments?

STEP 1: IDENTIFY THE TRIGGER MOMENTS

What sparks the need for your solution? What **situation, event, or emotion** pushes your ideal client to search for an answer?

Triggers can be grouped into three categories:

1. Knowable Triggers (Directly Identifiable)

These are situations where you can pinpoint *exactly* who is experiencing them. You can even make a list of potential customers.

Examples:

- A startup just raised funding and now needs a branding agency.
- A homeowner just bought a house and needs home insurance.
- A company just posted a job opening for a CMO—likely needing marketing services.

Your strategy: Run **targeted campaigns** directly at these people.

2. Recognizable Triggers (Self-Identification)

You can't directly identify these customers, but if you describe their situation, they will recognize themselves.

Examples:

- A company struggling with bad online reviews needs reputation management.
- A business owner feeling overwhelmed by their workload needs automation tools.
- A marketer frustrated with low engagement needs a new strategy.

Your strategy: Create **topical campaigns** that highlight these moments, so customers see themselves and self-select.

3. Learnable Triggers (Education Required)

These are problems your audience doesn't know they have yet. You must educate them before they even realize they need you.

Examples:

- A company losing customers due to poor onboarding might not recognize the issue until it's pointed out.
- A freelancer underpricing their services may not realize they're undervaluing themselves.
- A business relying on word-of-mouth may not see the importance of SEO.

Your strategy: Use **content marketing** to educate them on the problem—and position yourself as the solution.

STEP 2: DESIGN THE RIGHT CAMPAIGN FOR EACH TRIGGER

Trigger Type	Marketing Approach	Why It Works
Knowable	**Targeted Campaigns** (Direct outreach, personalized ads)	Higher conversion since you know exactly who needs you.
Recognizable	**Topical Campaigns** (Ads, social media posts, relatable stories)	Customers see themselves and take action.
Learnable	**Content Marketing** (Blogs, webinars, guides)	Educates people into becoming future customers.

Each type requires a different marketing approach—but when you get it right, your marketing feels more like **help** and less like a sales pitch.

ASK AI TRIGGERS

Your ideal client:

- What situation, event, or emotion triggers the need for this solution?
- Who is most likely experiencing this problem right now?

Ask your favorite AI chat bot.

Get the Prompt

Get the prompt. Copy, paste, adapt and run.

FINAL THOUGHT: BE THERE WHEN IT COUNTS

Most marketing fights for attention when customers **aren't** ready to buy. But when you use trigger marketing, you show up when they **are** ready.

So, what are the key trigger moments for your business? Find them, and you'll never have to "chase" customers again.

Trigger Marketing canvas

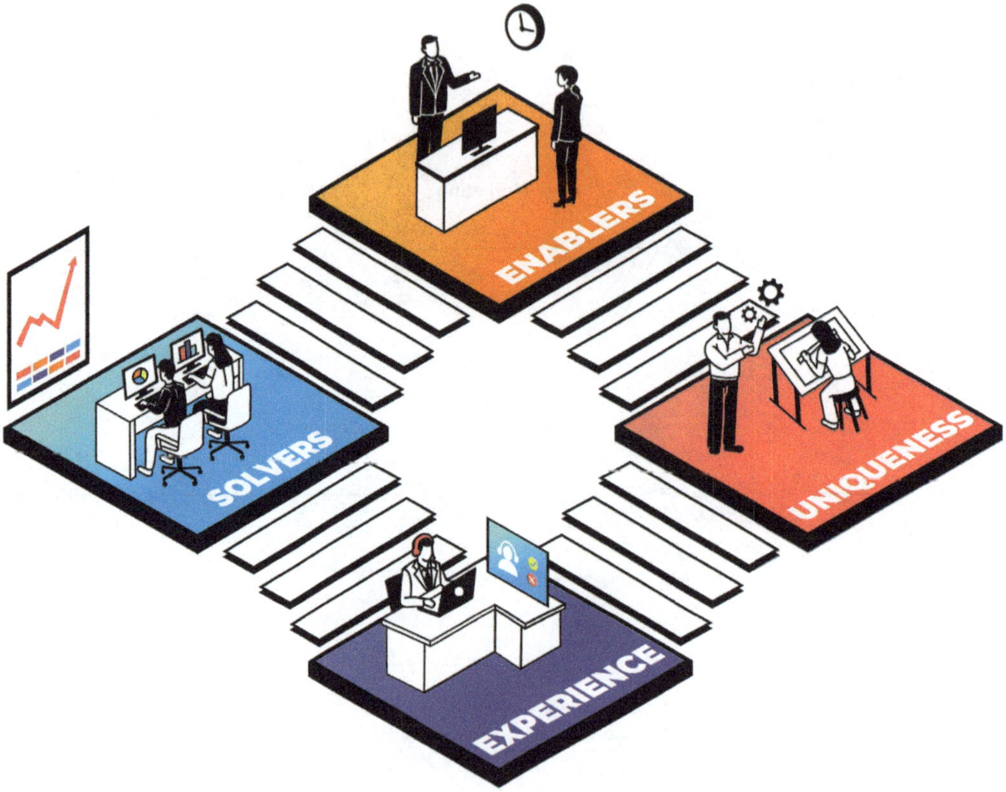
ENABLERS
SOLVERS
UNIQUENESS
EXPERIENCE

YOUR ORGANIZATION (COMPANY) 10

Take a hard look on your organization.

Most companies define themselves by **what they do**—their products, their services, their internal processes. But customers don't care about organizational charts or feature lists. They care about **what's in it for them**.

It's time to shift perspectives. Instead of looking from the **inside-out**, take a few steps and turn around to take an **outside-in approach**. How does your organization appear from your customer's standpoint? What do they actually experience?

Instead of looking from the inside-out, take a few steps and turn around to take an outside-in approach.

To do this, we'll break your organization down into **key building blocks**—each one designed to keep your customer at the center:

Enablers - Features that help your customers achieve their goal

Solvers - How you solve their problems

Experience – What is the journey like for your customer? How do they interact with you?

Uniqueness – Being *better* isn't enough. Being *different* is what sets you apart. What makes your company unique? Could you even define a **new category** that frames you as the only choice?

Brand Persona – People connect with brands that feel human. What traits define your brand? Are you bold? Trustworthy? Playful? Serious?

Extra Delight – Beyond solving problems, how do you make your customers' experience easier, smoother, or even *more enjoyable*?

Thinking about your organization this way transforms how you communicate, position yourself, and ultimately, how customers perceive you.

Let's step into their shoes and build a brand that resonates where it matters most.

Organization canvas

Organization (company)

standpoint

Enablers	Solvers	Experience
A	B	C

Uniqueness	Brand Persona	Extra Delight	Matching
D	E	F	G

©2024

WHAT YOU DO

Most companies talk about **what they do** in terms of features—lists of tools, services, and fancy jargon that sound impressive in a boardroom but don't mean much to customers. But here's the truth:

Customers don't buy features. They buy progress.

They are either trying to **achieve something** (*finally get in shape, grow their business, master sourdough baking*) or **escape something** (*feeling out of shape, struggling with a stagnant business, constantly making flat bread when it should be fluffy*).

And here's where your business comes in:

- **Enablers** help customers move forward toward a goal (positive emotions: ambition, excitement, progress).
- **Solvers** help customers remove an obstacle (negative emotions: frustration, fear, anger, stress).

And the best part? **Your business does both.**

Every company enables and solves at the same time—it's just a matter of how your customer sees it.

- Some people want to "get fit" (an aspiration—an Enabler).
- Others just want to "stop feeling sluggish" (fixing a problem—a Solver).

Same product, different mindset. If you understand both perspectives, you can craft a message that clicks with your audience—whether they're running toward something or *away* from it (possibly literally).

A. Enablers: Helping Customers Move Forward

Enablers empower customers to **reach their aspirations**. They make progress easier, faster, or more effective. These products and services are associated with *hope, motivation, and the dream of finally getting their life together.*

Enablers empower customers to reach their aspirations.

Examples of Enablers:

- A **language-learning app** that helps users become fluent (so they can finally impress their in-laws).
- A **fitness program** that guides people toward a healthier lifestyle (without forcing them to eat only kale).
- A **business consulting firm** that helps companies scale efficiently (so they can stop making it up as they go along).

Ask Yourself:

- What does my customer want to accomplish?
- How does my product or service make it happen?

Think of the difference between "main" features and "complementary" features. The first are the core of your offer. Often the later ones are added to solve a problem or to enhance the experience.

Movie theater

Let's take a movie theater as an example.

The room and a place to sit, maybe also. Things like popcorn and extra comfy leather seats are secondary.

Write up what you do, what you deliver to your customer that helps them accomplish their aspiration.

ASK AI ENABLERS

Your ideal client:

- What part of your offer helps your customers accomplish their aspirations, reach their goals?

Ask your favorite AI chat bot.

Get the prompt ◀ ***Get the prompt.*** Copy, paste, adapt and run.

B. Solvers: Removing Roadblocks & Pain Points

Solvers eliminate **problems, frustrations, or inefficiencies** standing in the way of progress. They aren't dreaming of a brighter future; they're just trying to make today suck less.

These solutions bring *relief, reassurance, and the satisfaction of finally fixing that one annoying thing.*

Solvers eliminate problems, frustrations, or inefficiencies

Examples of Solvers:

- **A password manager** that eliminates security headaches (because no one actually remembers their passwords).
- **A legal service** that simplifies business compliance (so entrepreneurs can stop having nightmares about paperwork).
- **A pain relief medication** that helps people function without discomfort (because "powering through" is not a real health plan).

Ask Yourself:

- What's stopping my customer from reaching their goal?
- What frustration, risk, or inefficiency do I eliminate?

Pro Tip: Listen to how customers talk about their needs:

- If they say, "*I want to be more productive,*" they're looking for an Enabler.
- If they say, "*I'm sick of wasting time,*" they need a Solver.

Write up what you do, what you deliver that helps the customer solve a problem, remove an obstacle, relieve a pain.

Movie theater

Back in the day, you would show up a half an hour early, wait in line to buy your ticket and then go pick your seat and wait. You didn't want to end up in the front row. Now, you can buy your ticket online and pick your seat in advance. This way, you can show up at the last minute and have your perfect seat free for you. This is the solution to a problem, a complementary feature.

This can be an inspiration for new features that solve specific problems, such as the "having to go early to the movie theater".

ASK AI SOLVERS

Your ideal client:

- What part of your offer helps your customers tackle their challenges, solve their problems?

Ask your favorite AI chat bot.

Get the Prompt ◀ ***Get the prompt.*** Copy, paste, adapt and run.

HOW IT WILL HAPPEN

Customers worry about what it will be like.

Worry isn't good.

> ***Customers worry about what it will be like. Worry isn't good.***

C. Experience

Your customers don't just care about what you offer—they care about **what it's like to work with you**. And if the experience feels like climbing a bureaucratic mountain in flip-flops, they're not sticking around.

So, let's make it simple.

The experience has two big questions customers subconsciously ask:

- How easy is it to get started? (*"Can I actually do this?"*)
- What will the whole experience be like? (*"Will this be smooth or a headache?"*)

Your job? **Answer both in a way that makes them think, "Oh, that's simple. I can do that. That will be good."**

Make It Easy to Get Started

What's the purchase or onboarding experience like?

Customers should feel like they're stepping onto an escalator, not solving a Rubik's Cube blindfolded.

Ask Yourself:

- Can I summarize the process in **3 simple steps**?
- Is it easy to understand, test, and adopt?
- What's the *very next thing* I want them to do?

Example 3-Step Processes:

Music Discovery Service:

1. Create an account.
2. Select 5 of your favorite bands.
3. Discover new music you'll love.

ERP Software (even SAP, the king of complexity):

1. We analyze your company.
2. We configure everything using our proven methodology.
3. We roll out seamlessly and level up your business.

E-Commerce Store:

1. Pick your product.
2. One-click checkout.
3. Get it delivered fast.

Why 3 Steps?

Because our brains love threes. It's just the right amount of information to feel **structured but not overwhelming**. More than three, and it starts feeling like an instruction manual for assembling furniture.

The Goal: Make them think: *"That sounds easy. I can do that."*

The Full Experience: What's It Like Over Time?

Once they've started, they still have **big questions about the road ahead**:

- Will the purchase go smoothly? (Or will I be forced to make an account, verify my email, enter a captcha, and do a backflip before I can buy?)
- Is it easy to install or set up? (Or do I need an engineering degree?)
- Will they guide me, or am I on my own?
- What happens if I get stuck? How fast will they help?
- Is there a money-back guarantee? A safety net?
- Can they do it for me if I don't want to deal with it?
- How long will this last? Will I need constant upgrades?

You don't need to answer all of these—just the ones that matter most for your offer.

Make It Clear How You're Different

People already have expectations for how things usually work in your industry. If you break the mold in a good way, highlight it.

Examples of Differentiation:

Car Buying Experience:

The old way: Painfully long negotiations at a dealership.

The new way: "Buy online. Delivered to your door. 7-day test drive."

Home Repair Service:

The old way: "We'll be there sometime between 8 AM and 8 PM."

The new way: "Track your technician in real time."

Meal Subscription Box:

The old way: "You're locked into a monthly plan."

The new way: "Pause or cancel anytime with one click."

Aha moments like these create positive emotions and build trust. They make the customer think, "*Oh! That's smart. I like that.*" And that's when they start leaning in.

Reduce Friction, Increase Engagement

If you make it **easy to try** and **rewarding to stay**, customers won't just buy—they'll stick around.

Andy Cars' Customer Happiness Canvas is a great resource for this. It focuses on two key things:

Customer Happiness Canvas

- **Reduce friction to getting new customers.** (Make it easy to try!)
- **Increase engagement and loyalty.** (Make them want to stay!)

Tactics That Work:

- Free trial with no credit card required. (So, they don't feel trapped.)
- Instant setup or guided onboarding. (Because no one wants to feel lost.)
- A simple, low-risk first step. (Instead of "commit now," offer "try first.")
- Ongoing engagement. (Surprise them with value over time—don't disappear after the sale.)

Make a Sequence of Key Moments in the Customer's Journey

Map out the **most important touchpoints** where your customers might hesitate, feel unsure, or wonder what's next. Then, make each of those moments **clear, simple, and reassuring.**

A good experience isn't just **smooth**—it's **predictable** in the best way. When customers know what to expect, they feel in control.

Final Thought: People Remember How You Made Them Feel

At the end of the day, your customers **won't remember every feature, price, or detail**. But they will remember how the experience **felt**.

If it was **simple, smooth, and enjoyable**, they'll **come back and tell others.**
If it was c**onfusing, frustrating, or felt like a chore**, they'll **avoid you like a bad Tinder date**.

So, how do you want them to feel? Make it easy. Make it enjoyable. Make them think:

"That was great. I'd do that again."

ASK AI EXPERIENCE

Your ideal client:

- What will the experience be like?

Ask your favorite AI chat bot.

Get the Prompt ◀ ***Get the prompt.*** Copy, paste, adapt and run.

WHAT MAKES YOU DIFFERENT

Different is better than better.

Different is better than better.

How do you stand out?

D. Uniqueness

How are you different? And I don't mean "**better, faster, cheaper**"—those are weak answers. Everyone claims to be better. Everyone says they're faster. Everyone wants to be cheaper *(until they realize it's a terrible business model)*.

True uniqueness is about **being different in a way that actually matters**. It's about taking a stand, challenging the status quo, and making people see your offer as **the only logical choice**.

So let's get specific.

Your Unique Point of View: What's Broken in Your Industry?

Every industry has an "**old way**" of doing things. And every truly unique brand introduces a **"new way."**

- **Peloton**: The old way? Dragging yourself to the gym. The new way? Live and on-demand workouts at home, with an instructor cheering you on.
- **Oura Ring:** The old way? Bulky fitness trackers that look like mini computers on your wrist. The new way? A sleek, stylish ring that tracks your sleep and health.
- **Liquid Death:** The old way? Boring plastic water bottles. The new way? Mountain water in tallboy cans, with punk rock branding that makes hydration feel hardcore.
- **Notion:** The old way? A dozen different apps for notes, tasks, and documents. The new way? One beautifully designed workspace to organize everything.

Your job is to **define the old way and show how your new way is a game-changer**.

Ask Yourself:

- What's outdated, annoying, or inefficient about the traditional approach?
- How does your way flip the script?
- What do you want to be **known for**?

If you can clearly communicate why your way is different (and better), people will remember you.

If not, you're just another option on a long list.

Niche Down. Then Niche Down Again.

One of the most common mistakes I see? **Trying to be everything to everyone**.

- "We serve small businesses, but also large enterprises!"
- "Our software works for any industry!"
- "We make pizza, sushi, and also tacos!" *(Please don't do this.)*

When you try to appeal to everyone, **no one cares.** You become forgettable.

The best brands **niche down** so they can dominate a specific space.
I tell every entrepreneur and executive I coach:
Pick a niche. Then cut it in half. Then cut it in half again.

It's far better to be **loved by 20 percent of the market and ignored by the rest than to be just another average option that no one cares about**.

Of course, don't niche down so much that your total market is **five people and a dog**. Find the balance.

Ask Yourself:

- What's the **one** group that will love you the most?
- How can you narrow your focus to serve them better than anyone else?
- What would make you the **obvious** choice for that niche?

Own Your Category: The Power of Category Design

Want to **win big** in your industry? Stop competing on someone else's terms. **Create a new category and own it**.

Category Design

This strategy is called Category Design, and it's what separates brands that dominate from brands that struggle for scraps.

Big-Name Examples:

- **Airbnb** owns the **home-sharing** category. Competitors have been around for **decades**, yet Airbnb still takes over 20 percent market share.
- **Zoom** didn't just enter the video conferencing space—it **became the verb** for online meetings.
- **Red Bull** owns the **energy drink** category. It has almost 50 percent market share and is the **third most valuable soft drink brand** after Coca-Cola and Pepsi.

Now, think about this:

Can you name three other energy drinks besides Red Bull?

Most people can't. **Even with almost 200 competitors**. That's how powerful category ownership is.

Local Example: How to Dominate in Geneva

There are a gazillion **pizzerias** in Geneva. If I wanted to open one, it wouldn't just be "another pizza place."

Instead, I'd open the **only** "Chicago Pizza" restaurant. For example.

Now, instead of people asking, *"Which pizzeria should we go to?"* they'll ask:

"Normal pizza or Chicago pizza?"

Boom. I just created my **own** category. And I'm the only player in it.

This works everywhere. Instead of competing, **shift the decision entirely** so customers have to pick between:

- The old way vs. your way.
- The traditional option vs. the bold new option.
- Everyone else vs. you.

Final Thought: Dare to Be Different

Most companies are **terrified** of taking a strong stance because they worry about excluding people.

But the truth is:

If you're for everyone, you're for no one.

Dare to be different. Stand for something. Create a category.

That's how you stop being **just another option** and start being the **only choice**.

ASK AI UNIQUENESS

Your ideal client:

- What makes your offer unique?
- How do you differentiate from the competition?

Ask your favorite AI chat bot.

Get the prompt. Copy, paste, adapt and run.

Get the Prompt

E. Brand Persona

You don't just sell a product or service—you represent **something bigger**. Customers don't just see a company; they see a **persona**—a character with a distinct style, voice, and attitude.

Customers don't just see a company; they see a persona.

And if you don't define it, they'll do it for you.

What Are Your Values? And Do You Live By Them?

Every brand claims to have values. But the real question is: **Do they match what you actually do?**

- If you say you're about **innovation**, but your processes are stuck in the '90s, that's a problem.
- If you say you value **customer care**, but your support is impossible to reach, people will notice.
- If you claim to be **fun and bold**, but your website looks like a corporate tax form, something's off.

Ask Yourself:

- What three core values define how we act?
- Would customers actually describe us this way?
- Are we showing these values or just saying them?

Your values should be **obvious in everything you do**, from your marketing to your customer service to the way you write an email.

What's Your Brand Archetype?

Every strong brand has a **recognizable personality**, and this is where **Brand Archetypes** come in.

- **The Hero:** Inspires people to push beyond their limits *(Nike, Adidas).*
- **The Rebel:** Breaks the rules and challenges the norm *(Harley-Davidson, Virgin).*
- **The Sage:** Provides wisdom and expertise *(Harvard, Google).*
- **The Caregiver:** Supports and nurtures *(Johnson & Johnson, Dove).*

Picking an archetype (or a mix of two) **helps guide your messaging** and how people emotionally connect with your brand.

Ask Yourself:

- Do I want to inspire, challenge, educate, or nurture?
- What brands do I admire, and what archetypes do they use?
- Does my current tone and style reflect this personality?

Go discover—or define—your **Brand Archetype**.

▶ *Brand Archetypes*

Style, Tone & Visual Identity: How Do You Show Up?

Your **words, visuals, and attitude** all shape how customers perceive you. If your brand were a person, how would it dress? How would it talk?

- **Casual & Friendly**: Like chatting with an old friend (Mailchimp, Innocent Drinks).
- **Luxury & Exclusive**: Polished, refined, and aspirational (Rolex, Chanel).
- **Quirky & Fun**: Playful, unexpected, and full of personality (Oatly, Old Spice).
- **Serious & Professional**: No fluff, just expertise (IBM, McKinsey).

Ask Yourself:

- Does my writing sound **consistent**, or does it change depending on the mood of the day?
- If my brand had a **dress code,** what would it be?
- Would my visuals stand out in my industry, or do they blend in?

Your **style and tone** should be recognizable **even without a logo**. If someone reads your content or sees your designs, they should *know* it's you.

Final Thought: You're Telling a Story—So Who's the Main Character?

Your **Brand Persona** is the character your business plays in your industry. It's not just about selling—**it's about how people experience you**.

If you don't define who you are, customers will make assumptions. And you might not like the ones they make.

So take control.

Decide how you want to be **seen, heard, and remembered**.

Then, **show up that way—everywhere**.

F. Extra Delight

Your core offer is important, but **delight** happens outside the features. It's not just what you sell - it's **how you make people feel** throughout the entire experience.

> ***It's not just what you sell - it's how you make people feel throughout the entire experience.***

Customers may come for the **solution**, but they stay for the **unexpected moments that make them smile, feel valued, or make their lives easier.**

Think about the businesses you're loyal to. It's probably not just because they do the job—it's because they **exceed expectations, make things effortless, or surprise you in a way you didn't see coming.**

So how do you build that into your brand?

Expectations: Set Them, Then Surpass Them

Much of how we experience a product or service comes down to expectations.

- A **five-star hotel** can feel disappointing if the service is mediocre.
- A **dingy food truck** can feel like an incredible find if the tacos are amazing.

One of the **fastest ways to create loyalty** is to consistently **over-deliver**—not by making wild promises, but by subtly exceeding what customers expect.

I once had an **Internet hosting service** solve an issue caused by a third-party vendor—not their responsibility at all. But they fixed it anyway. And now? I'd never go anywhere else.

Ask Yourself:

- What expectations do I set for my customers?
- Do I systematically meet or exceed them?
- Where can I add an unexpected moment of value?

Transformation: What Do They Become?

There's an old saying: **Customers don't buy products. They buy a transformation.**

People aren't just buying **things**—they're buying who they become because of them.

- **A gym membership** doesn't just give access to weights. It makes you someone who prioritizes health.
- **A kitchen knife** isn't just a tool. It makes you a better chef.
- **A to-do list app** isn't just software. It makes you an organized person.
- **A tailored suit** isn't just fabric. It makes you stand out as a professional.

Ask Yourself:

- What **identity shift** does my offer create?
- How can I emphasize this transformation in my messaging?
- What proof or moments can I create to make customers feel that shift sooner?

Transitions: Make Switching Painless

People often stick with **imperfect solutions** because switching feels like a headache.

- Ever considered changing **hairdressers** but didn't want to explain your style to someone new?
- Ever thought about **switching banks** but dreaded the paperwork?
- Ever wanted to try a **new software tool** but felt overwhelmed at the idea of learning it?

Switching costs are real. Even if your offer is better, customers may hesitate if the **transition seems painful**.

Ask Yourself:

- What barriers make switching difficult?
- How can I make onboarding effortless?
- Can I offer white-glove setup, an easy transfer process, or a risk-free trial?

The easier you make the switch, the faster you win customers.

Interaction: Make Every Touchpoint Effortless (or Even Fun)

Few things are more frustrating than **bad customer interactions**.

- Waiting on hold forever.
- Repeating your issue to five different agents.
- Digging through endless FAQs to find an answer.

If **interacting with you is smooth, fast, or—dare I say—enjoyable**, customers will remember that.

Ask Yourself:

- How can I simplify how customers reach me?
- Can I make my website, checkout, or support process seamless?
- Is there a way to add a touch of personality or humor to interactions?

Companies like **Mailchimp** and **Innocent Drinks** have built entire brand personalities around making even **error messages and customer service fun**. It works.

Testing: Let Customers Try Before They Buy

People hesitate before making a decision. The more **risk-free** it feels, the faster they'll move forward.

Ask Yourself:

- Can I offer a free trial, sample, or demo?
- If I sell physical products, can I offer a try-at-home option?
- How can I give potential customers a taste of value before they commit?

Testing makes people **comfortable** - and comfort leads to sales.

Quick Wins: Show Value Fast

A major factor in customer **satisfaction and retention** is **time to value**—how long it takes for them to see real results.

Nobody wants to wait months to feel like they made a good decision.

- **Duolingo** gives you a first **successful lesson** in minutes.
- **Peloton** makes you feel like an athlete after **one engaging ride**.
- **Trello** lets you set up a board and feel **instantly organized**.

The **faster customers feel progress**, the more likely they'll stick with you.

Ask Yourself:

- What **quick win** can I give customers right away?
- How can I **shorten the time between signup and success**?
- Can I create a **moment of progress in the first 5 minutes**?

The Extended Experience: Surprise & Delight Moments

Some of the best customer experiences come from **small, unexpected touches**.

- Some coffee shops strategically place outlets so remote workers and students choose them over competitors. It costs next to nothing, but keeps people coming back.
- A few comfy chairs and a warm atmosphere make people stay longer, increasing the chances they'll buy a book.
- A $0.50 coffee makes a customer feel like they're in a premium environment and reinforces the brand's exclusivity.

These little extras stick in people's minds.

Ask Yourself:

- What **small touch** could improve the experience?
- How can I make my service **more comfortable, convenient, or enjoyable**?
- Is there a way to **surprise customers with something they didn't expect**?

A **handwritten thank-you note** in a package. A **bonus upgrade** they didn't see coming. These little efforts don't just create **customers**—they create **fans**.

Final Thought: The Best Businesses Don't Just Deliver—They Delight

Customers expect you to **do what you promised**. That's the baseline. But if you go beyond that—**if you surprise them, make things easy, and create moments they remember**—they won't just buy from you.

They'll **talk about you, stay with you, and come back again and again**.

The businesses that **master extra delight** don't have to fight for attention.

They get it naturally.

ASK AI EXTRAS

Your ideal client:

- What do you do or what could you do to enhance add extra delight to their experience?

Ask your favorite AI chat bot.

Get the prompt ◀ ***Get the prompt.*** Copy, paste, adapt and run.

REALITY CHECK

Matching

After analyzing your customer's **aspirations, challenges, and triggers**, ask yourself:

Does your offer actually meet their most important needs—or are you just assuming it does?

Focus on the Right Problems

Trying to solve everything leads to **mediocrity**. The best companies **choose** what to solve—and what to ignore.

Ask Yourself:

- Are we **solving what matters most** or just adding features?
- Would **removing** some features make our offer **stronger**?

Small Changes, Big Impact

Often, **small tweaks** can dramatically improve fit.

Examples:

- A software tool adding an essential integration.
- A subscription service letting customers pause instead of cancel.
- A consulting firm offering a free onboarding session.

Ask Yourself:

- What **quick, low-cost improvements** could enhance customer experience?
- Are we **overcomplicating things** when a simple fix would work?

Prioritize What Matters

Not all ideas are worth pursuing. Choose the ones that:

- Have the biggest impact on your ideal customer.
- Fit naturally into your strengths.
- Avoid wasting effort on low-value changes.

Ask Yourself:

- Are we **staying true** to our brand or chasing shiny objects?
- If we could **only pick three improvements**, what would they be?

Final Thought: Alignment Over More

You don't need **more features**—you need **better fit**.

- Solve the right problems.
- Keep it simple.
- Prioritize what truly moves the needle.

When your offer aligns **perfectly** with customer needs, you're no longer just an option—you're the **only choice**.

ACKNOWLEDGMENT

VPC Inspiration ◀

Before developing my own canvases, my go to framework was the **Value Proposition Design canvas** by Alex Osterwalder and Yves Pigneur.

The "Organization (company)" canvas is similar to the right side.

Check out how I was inspired.

EXAMPLES

Part 5—on P. 209—has a long list of examples of the four steps of Storybuilding. Here are three examples of the Organization canvas to give you an idea.

B2C: Subscription Boxes for Self-Care and Wellness (P. 232)

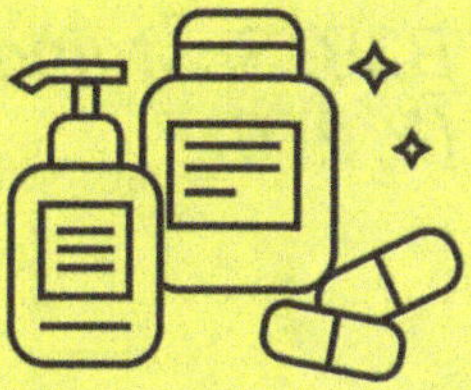

Organization (company)

standpoint

Enablers

- A selection of premium self-care items, such as candles, skincare, bath salts, and mindfulness tools
- Ability to personalize boxes based on preferences or needs (e.g., stress relief, energy boost)
- Guides and tips included in each box for maximizing the benefits of the products

Solvers

- Auto-delivery of monthly boxes saves customers time and effort
- Partnering with wellness experts to vet products ensures quality and effectiveness
- Biodegradable and sustainable materials to ease eco-conscious concerns

Experience

- The subscription model ensures seamless delivery
- Ability to personalize their boxes based on their needs, such as stress relief or energy boosts
- The surprise bonus item in every box and the occasional self-care challenges
- Exclusive access to forums or apps allows them to share experiences and tips

Uniqueness

- Focuses on both physical and mental well-being, blending mindfulness tools with skincare and wellness products
- Prioritizes ethical and sustainable sourcing for all products
- Offers a "pause anytime" subscription option to reduce commitment anxiety

Brand Persona

- Warm, nurturing, and empowering - a "best friend" who helps you prioritize yourself
- Tone emphasizes encouragement and positivity
- Modern yet cozy, using soft colors and clean design

Extra Delight

- A surprise "bonus item" in every box
- Monthly self-care challenges (e.g., "30 days of mindfulness")
- Access to a community forum: subscribers can connect, share tips, and learn

Matching

©2024

B2B: Sustainable Office Supplies for Small Businesses (P. 250)

Organization (company)

standpoint

Enablers

- A one-stop shop for eco-friendly office essentials (e.g., recycled paper, biodegradable pens)
- Products clearly labeled with trusted eco-certifications (e.g., FSC, Fair Trade)
- Monthly deliveries of commonly used supplies tailored to office needs

Solvers

- Cost-competitive options that make sustainability accessible for small businesses
- Programs for recycling used office supplies, such as paper and ink cartridges
- Guides and workshops on creating a greener office environment

Experience

- Comprehensive catalog of eco-certified products
- Subscription services for regular deliveries of essential supplies
- Personalized Sustainability Impact Reports
- Workshops and guides

Uniqueness

- Focuses exclusively on eco-friendly office supplies with end-to-end sustainability
- Offers a recycling buyback program where customers can return used products for discounts
- Partners with local green businesses for exclusive offerings

Brand Persona

- Friendly, knowledgeable, and committed to sustainability
- Clean and earthy branding with a focus on simplicity and authenticity

Extra Delight

- Exclusive loyalty rewards for eco-conscious customers (e.g., discounts for recycling old supplies).
- A quarterly "Green Office Box" with curated sustainable products to inspire employees

Matching

©2024

Peer-to-Peer Rental Marketplace (P. 268)

Organization (company) Sellers Buyers

Enablers

Sellers	Buyers
Set availability, pricing, and rental terms for their items	Handmade, unique items with detailed artisan stories
Protection against damage or theft during rentals	Wishlists and receiving tailored recommendations
Real-time tracking of income and rental activity	Clear information on eco-certifications and fair-trade practices

Solvers

Sellers	Buyers
Payments processed securely and promptly	Buyer protection policies for peace of mind
Customer support for item damage or late returns	Guarantees that all items are genuinely handmade
Help sellers adjust pricing based on demand or trends	Customizable gift packaging and direct delivery

Experience

Sellers	Buyers
Tools for uploading and managing items: photo tips and templates	Updates on support to artisans and their communities
Chat to coordinate with renters and address inquiries	Live workshops, Q&A sessions, and virtual studio tours
Notifications about bookings, reviews, and earnings	Exclusive access to rare and seasonal collections

Uniqueness

Sellers	Buyers
High-demand items like event equipment & tools	Creator's background and inspiration
Sustainability by encouraging sharing over new purchases	Handmade goods only
	Sustainability and ethical sourcing

Brand Persona

Sellers	Buyers
Empowering	Thoughtful and Creative
Resourceful	Inclusive and Transparent
Trustworthy	Supportive of Individuality

Extra Delight

Sellers	Buyers
Discounts on platform fees for frequent sellers	Earn rewards for every purchase
Earnings and environmental contribution dashboard	Curated lists for holidays or milestones
Highlight successful sellers in newsletters or social media	Seamless integration for showcasing purchases

Matching

©2024

SIDE QUEST: YOUR CATEGORY

B

If you don't define your **category**, the market will—and you might not like the results.

The strongest brands don't just compete; they **own a space**. Red Bull owns energy drinks, Airbnb appropriated home-sharing, and Zoom became the verb for video calls. Instead of fighting for market share, they **reframed the conversation** to make themselves the obvious choice.

HOW ARE YOU DIFFERENT?

Market Positioning: Where Do You Fit?

Your first job is to clearly define where you belong - or carve out a space where you stand alone.

- What category are you in? Could you **define a new one**?
- If a customer had to put you in a **bucket**, what would it be?
- What's the **traditional way** of doing things in your industry?
- How is your approach **different from the norm**?
- If you disappeared tomorrow, what **gap** would be left in the market?

If your answer sounds like what everyone else is saying, you don't own a category—you're just competing in one.

Customer Perception: What Do They See?

Customers don't see your brand the way you do. The way they describe you is more important than how you describe yourself.

- What do your **most loyal customers** say they love about you?
- How do new customers describe you when they first find you?
- What emotional connection do customers have with your brand? (**Trust? Fun? Exclusivity?**)
- What's the biggest reason customers **choose you over competitors**?

Competitive Landscape: Why You, Not Them?

Standing out doesn't mean **doing everything better**—it means being **clearly different** in a way that matters.

- Who are your **top three competitors**, and how are they perceived?
- What do they do **well** that you don't? What do you do well that **they don't**?
- What's something you offer that your competitors **can't or won't**?
- Is there a **pain point competitors ignore** that you address?
- If a customer was comparing options, what's the **strongest argument** for choosing you?

Brand Identity: What's Your "Only"?

A strong brand isn't just better—it's **the only** one doing something specific.

- Can you complete this sentence? *"We're the only company that ____."*
- What's your **boldest opinion** about your industry?
- What values drive your company, and are they obvious in your **customer experience**?
- What's something **non-negotiable** about how you operate?
- If you had to **double down on one thing** that makes you different, what would it be?

Bonus: The "Gut Check" Questions

If you're still not sure what makes you stand out, try these:

- What do you want to be **famous for**?
- If a competitor copied everything you do, what's the **one thing they couldn't replicate**?
- If you had to remove **half your features/services**, what would still make you valuable?

FINAL THOUGHT: COMPETE LESS, OWN MORE

Your category isn't just about where you fit—it's about making sure you **own the conversation** in your space.

- If you're just fighting to be *better*, you'll always have competition.
- If you're **different in a way that matters**, customers won't compare - you'll be the obvious choice.

So, what's your category? And more importantly, do you own it?

ASK AI EXTRAS

Your ideal client:

- What is your category considering market positioning, customer perception, competitive landscape, and brand identity?

Ask your favorite AI chat bot.

Get the Prompt ◀ ***Get the prompt.*** Copy, paste, adapt and run.

PART 4:
STORYBUILDING

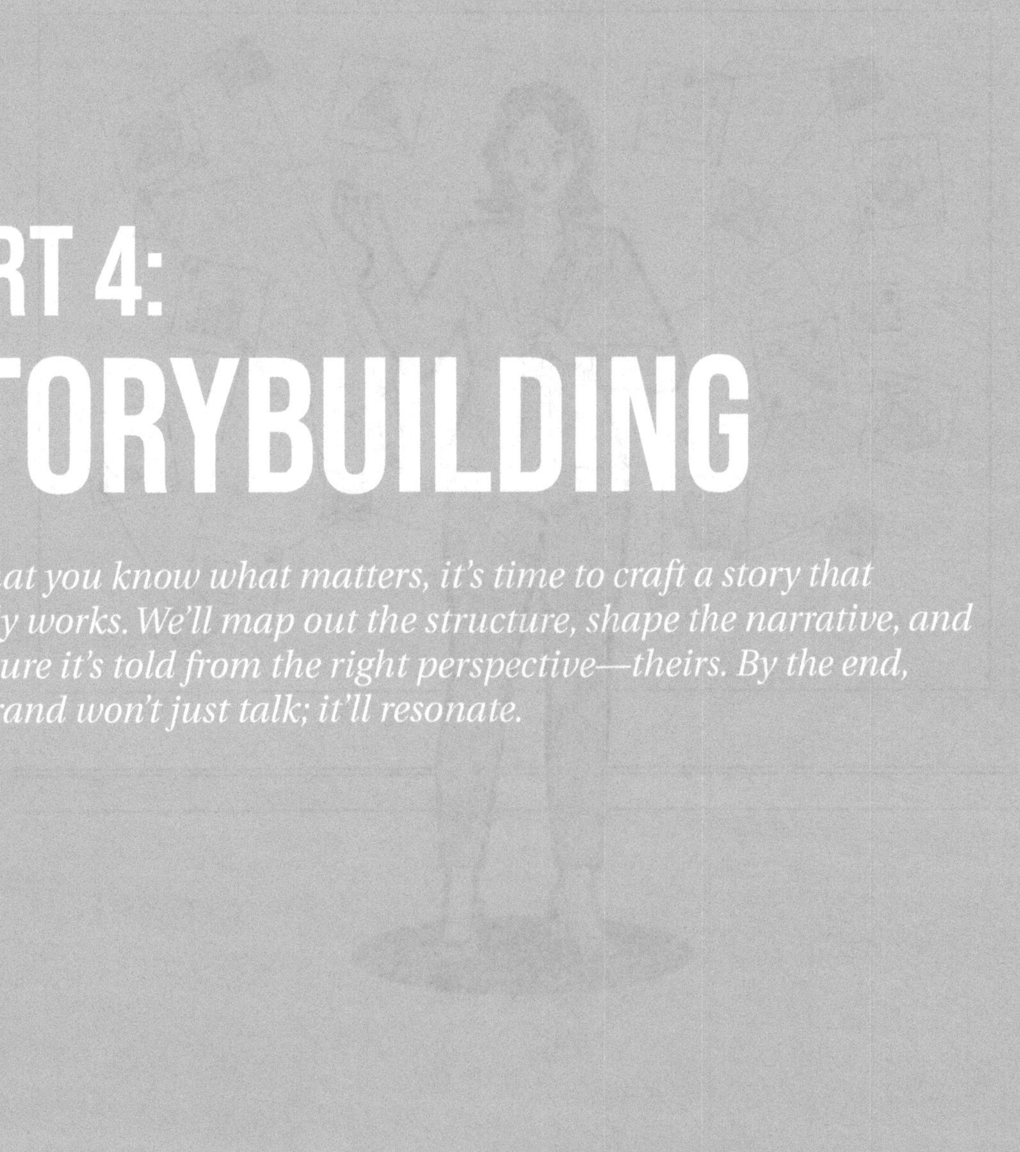

Now that you know what matters, it's time to craft a story that actually works. We'll map out the structure, shape the narrative, and make sure it's told from the right perspective—theirs. By the end, your brand won't just talk; it'll resonate.

STORYBUILDING FRAMEWORK

11

Decide what is important and put the pieces in an engaging sequence.

Now that you've gathered all the pieces, it's time to start shaping the **structure** of your story. Each element ties back to insights from the previous canvases, helping you craft a narrative that truly resonates with your audience.

Your job here isn't to include everything—it's to **choose wisely**. Among all the aspirations, challenges, triggers, and ideas you've identified, what will connect most **deeply** with your customer?

- Sometimes, it's a big-picture aspiration that draws them in.
- Other times, it's a small, daily frustration they desperately want to fix.

What's the strongest emotional hook you can use?

Prioritizing What Matters Most

There's a lot to work with, but not everything carries the same weight. That's why **Aspirations and Challenges appear twice** in the framework:

- **The most important ones come first**—these are the foundation of your story.
- **The secondary ones appear under Stakes and Positive Future**, reinforcing the emotional depth.

For now, don't worry about crafting perfect sentences. Focus on selecting the **key ideas**—the ones that will shape the story **your customers will actually care about**.

Storybuilding canvas

Storybuilding

standpoint

Recognition (me = stakeholder)	**First impression** E	**Stakeholder** 2	**Aspirations (Jobs)** 3	**Challenges (Pains)** 4
Perception (them = organization)	**Standpoint** D	**Category** D	**Values & Trust** 5CE	**Solution** AB
Projection (future me)	**Experience** C	**Transformation** F	**Stakes** 4B	**Positive future** 3A

©2024

THE THREE STEPS: RECOGNITION, PERCEPTION AND PROJECTION

In the first part of this book, we explored the **three steps** a customer goes through when encountering a brand:

1. **Recognition** – Deciding if it's "for them".
2. **Perception** – Understanding your offer and how you are different.
3. **Projection** – Imagining the positive future you promise.

Now, it's time to build a story that guides your audience through these steps - delivering the **right information, at the right moment, in the right sequence for maximum engagement**.

Using what you've learned about your **customer and organization**, you'll fill in this canvas with the most relevant insights from previous exercises.

At this stage, **bullet points are enough** - the goal is to create a **strong structure** before refining the actual wording. The clearer the framework, the more compelling the final story will be.

Let's go through these steps.

RECOGNITION

The first step in crafting your story is **recognition**—helping your target audience see themselves in your message. If they don't immediately feel like **this is for them**, they'll tune out.

If they don't immediately feel like this is for them, they'll tune out.

Your goal is to **select and refine** the customer, aspiration, and challenge that will create an instant connection. **Who are they? What do they want? What's in their way?**

This is where your story begins.

First Impression: The Emotional Hook

Before a word is read, before a customer understands what you do, they feel something about your brand. That first impression is powerful.

Even though it's not a formal part of the story, it **shapes the tone** and **frames their expectations**.

Ask Yourself:

- What **emotion** should they feel the moment they encounter you?
- What **vibe** do you want to create? Friendly? Expert? Bold? Reassuring?
- How does your **visual identity** (colors, design, images) reinforce this?
- What tone should your copy have—conversational, professional, playful?

This isn't just about looking good—it's about making sure the **first second of engagement** signals to the right people: *"You're in the right place."*

In the context of this canvas, what's important is to have this in mind for the rest of the exercise.

Stakeholder / Customer: Making It Clear Who You Serve

Your ideal customer should **immediately recognize themselves** in your message. The key is **balance**—specific enough to create recognition, but not so narrow that you exclude a huge portion of your audience.

If you try to appeal to **everyone**, no one will feel truly seen. If you go too **niche** (hard to do), you risk missing potential customers.

A Few Examples, from Broad to Specific:

Indoor Gardening Kits for Small Spaces:

- Everybody *(too broad)*
- Apartment renters *(better)*
- Young urban dwellers *(more targeted)*
- Students in dorms *(very specific, but limits reach)*

Online Skills Training and Career Development:

- Everybody (too broad)
- Workers (still too vague)
- Career switchers (more focused)
- Early-career professionals (stronger connection)
- Fresh graduates (very specific, but excludes mid-career workers)

It's okay to **combine a couple of segments** if they naturally fit.

IT Support for Co-Working Spaces:

- Co-working space managers (a perfect fit—this one is obvious!)

Other examples of clear, yet flexible customer groups:

- **Small businesses in food production**, packaging, and delivery.
- **Teachers, educators, and private tutors.**
- **Banks, financial advisors, and family offices.**

The key question: *How do you make them feel that this is for them?*

- Does your language reflect their world?
- Are you using situations and examples that they relate to?
- Do you specialize in working with people like them?

Your story should leave **no doubt** in their minds that they're in the right place.

ASK AI RECOGNITION/STAKEHOLDER

Your ideal client:

- How would you describe yourself so that you would immediately recognize yourself as their ideal customer?

Ask your favorite AI chat bot.

Get the prompt. Copy, paste, adapt and run.

Get the Prompt

Aspirations (Jobs): Connecting to What They Want

People engage with brands that help them move **toward something they want**.

You've identified **a range of customer aspirations**—now it's time to **choose the one that will resonate most**. It should:

- **Be relatable** to your audience.
- **Create contrast** with their challenges.
- **Show that you truly understand them.**

Some aspirations are **direct and explicit**:

- "Small companies looking to expand internationally…"
- "As parents, you want to choose the right foods for your newborn…"

Others are **more subtle but still powerful**:

- "As an inspiring leader, you…"
- "As a good parent, you…"

What to include:

- **Empathy signals** ("We understand you.")
- **Their core aspiration** (growth, success, security, happiness, freedom).
- **The emotions behind it** (confidence, pride, relief, excitement).

The best aspirations **don't just describe an end goal—they make the customer feel seen.**

ASK AI RECOGNITION/ASPIRATIONS

Your ideal client:

- What are your main aspirations in the scope of this offer?

Ask your favorite AI chat bot.

Get the prompt. Copy, paste, adapt and run.

▶ *Get the Prompt*

Challenges (Pains): Acknowledging Their Struggles

People don't just seek **aspirations**—they also need help overcoming **challenges**.

If you want customers to trust you, you have to show that you **understand their frustrations, obstacles, and pain points**.

Again, you've identified many potential challenges—your job now is to **pick the one that best connects** with your chosen aspiration.

Ask Yourself:

- What's the **biggest** struggle they face?
- What problem are they **most eager to fix**?
- How do they **feel** about this challenge?

Some challenges are practical:

- "Finding affordable ways to expand internationally."
- "Figuring out which foods are actually good for their baby."

Some are **emotional or identity-based**:

- "Worrying they aren't a good leader."
- "Feeling guilty about not spending enough time with their kids."

What to include:

- The **specific problem** or **obstacle** they face.
- The **emotional weight** that comes with it (stress, frustration, fear, doubt).

When a customer sees their **own struggle reflected in your story**, they know they're in the right place.

ASK AI RECOGNITION/CHALLENGES

Your ideal client:

- What are your main challenges and negative emotions linked to the scope of this offer?

Ask your favorite AI chat bot.

Get the Prompt

◀ ***Get the prompt.*** Copy, paste, adapt and run.

Recognition is the First Hook

If a potential customer doesn't **see themselves** in your story, they won't stick around for the rest.

- Make the **first impression** feel right.
- Ensure they **immediately recognize** that this is for them.
- Speak to **what they want** and **what's standing in their way**.

Get this right, and they won't just read on—they'll feel **invested** in what you have to say next.

PERCEPTION

Once customers recognize themselves in your story, they move to the next phase: deciding whether they trust you, respect you, and—most importantly—actually understand what you offer.

This is where the brain kicks in. They're thinking:

- **What is their posture, their difference?** (*Are they boldly challenging the status quo, or just another "we're the best" company blending into the noise?*)
- **What do I compare them to?** (*Are they a free app or a virtual senior consultant?*)
- **Do I trust and respect them?** (*Do they seem like experts, or do they give off "just watched a YouTube tutorial" energy?*)
- **Can I work with them?** (*Would this be a smooth partnership, or am I signing up for a long-term headache?*)
- **Do I even understand what they're offering?** (*Is this crystal clear, or do I need a translator to figure out what they actually do?*)

If you don't **define how they see you**, they'll do it themselves—and not always in a way that works in your favor.

Standpoint: What's Your Unique View on the Industry?

Customers don't just buy **products**—they buy **perspectives**.

A strong brand takes a stand. It has a **clear standpoint** on the problem and **how it should be solved**.

One of the best ways to differentiate is to **challenge the status quo**:

- What's the "old way" of doing things? (*And why does it frustrate people?*)
- What's your "new way"? (*And why is it a game-changer?*)

Examples:

Old Way: "Flipping through a giant IKEA manual, trying to assemble furniture with that one weird wrench."

New Way: "Furniture that snaps together in minutes—no tools, no frustration."

Old Way: "Hunting for parking, circling the block for 20 minutes."

New Way: "Book a parking spot in advance and drive straight in."

Old Way: "Taking notes in a million different notebooks and never finding them again."

New Way: "One smart app to organize all your thoughts, searchable in seconds."

Ask Yourself:

- What outdated **tradition, system, or process** drives you nuts?
- How does your approach **flip the script** and make life easier for your customers?
- What's the **one belief** that drives how you do things?

Positioning yourself **against** something can make it easier for customers to understand what you stand **for**.

ASK AI PERCEPTION/STANDPOINT

Your company:

- What is your unique view on the industry?

Ask your favorite AI chat bot.

Get the prompt. Copy, paste, adapt and run.

▶ *Get the Prompt*

Category: Where Do You Belong?

If people put you in the **wrong category**, you lose.

Customers **naturally categorize** products and services. They compare new things to what they already know. If they put you in the wrong bucket, they'll either misunderstand you or compare you to the wrong competitors (with the associated pricing preconception).

You must **define your own space** before someone else does.

Ask Yourself:

- What category do I want to be in?
- What do I want them to compare me to?
- Do I fit into an existing category, or should I create a new one?

Examples:

- "We're not a mattress company—we're a sleep performance brand."
- "We don't sell gym memberships—we offer personal fitness experiences."
- "This isn't just software—it's your AI-powered business partner."

What to include:

- Your category (so they mentally place you correctly).
- Your unique differentiator (what makes you unlike anything else in that space).

ASK AI PERCEPTION/CATEGORY

Your company:

- What category are you in?
- What category do your customers put you in?

Ask your favorite AI chat bot.

Get the prompt. Copy, paste, adapt and run.

▶ *Get the Prompt*

Trust Signals & Value Matching: Why Should They Believe You?

People trust what they **see**, not just what you **say**.

If you want customers to believe you're the right choice, you have to **show** it.

How to Build Trust Quickly:

- **Social proof** – Customer testimonials, case studies, industry awards.
- **Authority symbols** – Credentials, experience, certifications, partnerships.
- **Transparency** – Clear pricing, guarantees, behind-the-scenes content.
- **Values alignment** – If your audience cares about ethics, sustainability, or innovation, highlight it.

Ask Yourself:

- How can **I show, not just tell** that I'm trustworthy?
- What credibility markers do I have (**awards, testimonials, partnerships**)?
- Do my values align with what **my customers care about**?

Examples:

- "Used by over 10,000 professionals across 50 countries."
- "As featured in Forbes, TechCrunch, and The Guardian."
- "Our mission: To make high-quality education accessible to all."

Trust is **earned** through what people see, not just what they hear.

Solution: Make Your Offer Instantly Clear

Confusion is the fastest way to lose a customer.

If people don't **quickly and clearly** understand what you do and how it helps them, they move on. Your solution should be described in **simple, direct terms**—no jargon, no fluff.

Ask Yourself:

- How can I explain my offer in **one clear sentence**?
- Does **my mom** understand what we do?
- What **problem does it solve**?
- What **benefits do they get** (not just features)?

Examples:

- "A meal delivery service designed for busy parents who want healthy, homemade meals without the prep time."
- "An AI-powered marketing assistant that automates content creation and ad targeting, so you grow your brand effortlessly."
- "A subscription-based legal service that gives startups unlimited legal advice for a fixed monthly fee."

What to include:

- Solution description (what you offer).
- Key benefits (why it matters).
- What you do and don't do (to prevent misunderstandings).

Final Thought: Make It Easy to Understand & Trust You

Perception isn't about **convincing**—it's about **clarity and trust.**

- Take a **strong stance** on what's broken in your industry.
- Make sure customers place you in the **right category**.
- Use **trust signals** to reinforce credibility.
- Explain your solution in the **simplest, most direct way possible**.

When your positioning is clear, customers don't just **see you**—they **understand and believe in you**.

PROJECTION

By now, your audience **recognizes** themselves in your story and has formed a **perception** of your brand. The last step? Helping them **project** themselves into a future where your product or service is part of their life.

This is where logic takes a backseat, and emotion takes the wheel. Customers aren't just asking, *"What does this do?"*—they're wondering, *"What will my life be like with this?"*

If you do this right, they won't just want your offer; they'll feel like they **need** it.

Experience: What Will It Be Like?

The decision isn't just about the outcome—it's about the **journey**.

> ***The decision isn't just about the outcome - it's about the journey.***

Customers worry:

- Will this be complicated?
- Will I regret this?
- Is this going to take forever?

Your job is to **reassure them** that the experience will be smooth, simple, even enjoyable.

Ask Yourself:

- How easy is it to get started?
- What support will they have along the way?
- Will they feel taken care of?

Examples:

- Sign up in minutes, no hassle.
- 24/7 support—real humans, no robots.
- Most users see results in their first week.

If it feels effortless, they'll move forward. If it feels overwhelming, they'll stall.

ASK AI PROJECTION/EXPERIENCE

Your company:

- What experience do you offer to your ideal customer?

Ask your favorite AI chat bot.

Get the prompt. Copy, paste, adapt and run.

Get the Prompt

Transformation: Who Will They Become?

People don't just buy products; they buy **identities**.

They want to see themselves as **smarter, healthier, more successful, more confident**—and your brand should help them get there.

Ask Yourself:

- What version of themselves do they want to be?
- How will your product help them get there?

Would they be a:

- **More efficient entrepreneur?** (Because they finally automated tasks.)
- **A better parent?** (Because they found the best baby food delivery service.)
- **A sharper professional?** (Because they signed up for that skills course.)

Make them **feel** the shift—so they want it now, not "someday."

ASK AI PROJECTION/TRANSFORMATION

Your company:

- What type of transformation do you promise?

Ask your favorite AI chat bot.

Get the Prompt

Get the prompt. Copy, paste, adapt and run.

Stakes

Let's address the elephant in the room: **what happens if they don't choose you?**

Nobody likes to dwell on worst-case scenarios, but customers need to feel the stakes. If their current situation isn't painful enough, why would they change?

Ask yourself:

- What struggles will continue if they don't act?
- What frustrations, inefficiencies, or missed opportunities will persist?
- What's the risk of waiting too long?

This isn't about fear-mongering—it's about **reminding them that the status quo isn't great either**.

Examples:

- Stop wasting hours every week on spreadsheets.
- Feel confident in your use of AI.
- No more yo-yo dieting. A real, lasting change.

Sometimes, people need a little nudge to realize they're standing in their own way.

These are the **Supporting Insights** as defined in the Stakeholders canvas (P. 80).

ASK AI PROJECTION/STAKES

Your company:

- What problems, worries do you alleviate?

Ask your favorite AI chat bot.

Get the Prompt

Get the prompt. Copy, paste, adapt and run.

Paint the Positive Future

Now, the fun part—help them **see** how their life will be better.

Help them see how their life will be better.

This isn't just listing features or benefits. It's about creating a vivid picture of **who they become** with your product or service in their corner.

Ask Yourself:

- How will they feel after using it?
- What changes will they notice first?
- How will others see them differently?

Examples:

- Imagine opening your inbox and seeing "New Customers" instead of spam.
- Picture yourself actually enjoying workouts because they fit your lifestyle.
- Imagine your business running smoothly, with more profit and less stress.

Use **sensory details** and **emotional triggers**—people connect more with a *vision* than a *list*.

Final Thought: Make It Impossible to Say No

Projection is **where decisions happen**.

At this stage, they should **feel** the contrast:

- The frustration of staying where they are.
- The excitement of stepping into a better future.

When they can **see themselves winning with you**, they won't just want your offer—they'll feel like they're missing out if they don't take action.

ASK AI PROJECTION/POSITIVE FUTURE

Your ideal client:

- What is the positive future that they promise?
- How will your life be better?

Ask your favorite AI chat bot.

Get the prompt. Copy, paste, adapt and run.

Get the Prompt

OVERVIEW: BRINGING IT ALL TOGETHER

You've mapped out your story. You've made decisions. Some are solid. Some are still in the *"hmm… does this make sense?"* stage.

That's fine. **This is a framework, not a religious doctrine.**

Not every box has to be filled. Not every section applies to every business. The goal is to create a **structured yet natural** story that actually works for you—without feeling like it was written by a committee.

Recognition: Making It Click

Your first job? **Make your audience feel like this was made for them.**

This usually happens through three elements:

- **Identity** (Who they are)
- **Aspirations** (What they want)
- **Challenges** (What's in their way)

But don't overthink it—you don't need to awkwardly force all three into every sentence. They often **blend naturally**.

Examples:

"As a caring father of a newborn, you worry about your child's sleep."

(Identity: father | Aspiration: caring | Challenge: sleep deprivation that makes coffee an essential food group.)

"Food packaging companies need to comply with strict regulations."

(Challenge + Aspiration combined: staying in business without drowning in red tape.)

The key is **instant recognition**—if your audience has to pause and decode your message, you've already lost them.

Perception: Framing How They See You

Trust is **always** important. But shared values? That depends.

You probably don't need a **deep ethical alignment** with your plumber (*"Tell me more about your stance on environmental sustainability before fixing my sink"*).

But if you're choosing a **financial advisor**, you might want to know if they believe in **ethical investing**, support **local businesses**, or won't funnel your money into **companies that go against your principles**.

Two key things shape **perception**:

- **Standpoint** (How do you see the industry? What's broken? What's your better way?)
- **Category** (What do people compare you to? Are you a premium option, a disruptor, or something entirely new? Are you in a new category?)

In theory, these are separate. In reality? They blur together. Be creative in how you present them. Your audience should think:

- "This makes sense."
- "I like how they do things."
- "They're exactly what I need."

If they're still thinking, *"Wait… what do they actually do?"* - go back and simplify.

Projection: Seeing Themselves in the Story

This is where your audience stops analyzing and starts **feeling**. They need to **see themselves in a future** where your product or service is making their life easier, better, or at the very least, **less annoying**.

- Some offers need **detailed explanations** (complex solutions, high commitment).
- Others thrive on **simplicity** (low-risk, easy to adopt, no instructions needed).

And **transformation**? It's powerful, but it doesn't always need to be spelled out. Sometimes, it's better implied.

Instead of saying:

"This will make you a more confident leader."

Try:

"Lead meetings without second-guessing every decision."

If your audience can **see themselves winning**, they're already halfway convinced.

Step Back: Does It Feel Right?

You've got the **structure** of your story. Now it's time to test it.

- Explain it to a **customer, colleague, or even your skeptical friend** who questions everything.
- Some parts may already flow like a great elevator pitch. Others may still be clunky.
- Try it out. How does it feel?

Ask yourself:

- Has your **understanding of your customer** changed?
- Does your value proposition **feel clearer**?
- Do you have **new marketing ideas** (or at least a better way to describe what you do at dinner parties)?

We'll tackle **copywriting** soon. But first—**are you happy with how this feels**?

Examples

Part 5—on P. 209—is packed with **real-life Storybuilding examples**.

To get a sense of how this works in practice, here are three completed **Storybuilding Canvas** examples. Take a look—you might find exactly what you need to push your story from *good* to *damn, that's compelling.*

Online Skills Training and Career Development Platform
(P. 237)

Storybuilding

standpoint

Recognition
(me = stakeholder)

Do I feel welcome?
Do they work with people like me?
Do they understand my situation, my problem?

The first phase is emotional.

Perception
(them = organization)

Can I work with them?
What is their standpoint?
What do I compare them to?
Do I trust them, respect them?
Do I understand their solution?

The second phase is more intellectual.

Projection
(future me)

What will it be like?
How will I feel? Will I be happy?
What will I avoid? What will I gain?

The third phase is emotional again.
Decisions are made more at an emotional level than an intellectual one.

First impression	Stakeholder	Aspirations (Jobs)	Challenges (Pains)
	Early-career professionals and career switchers seeking to advance or transition in their careers	Gain practical, job-ready skills, confidently transition into new roles, and build standout resumes	Struggling to identify in-demand skills, balance learning with responsibilities, and find accountability and guidance
Standpoint	**Category**	**Values & Trust**	**Solution**
Career development should be practical, flexible, and empowering. The old way of unstructured free resources or costly traditional programs is ineffective; the new way is efficient and tailored.	Online skills training and career development platform	Industry-aligned curriculum, recognized certificates, and mentorship from professionals	Flexible, affordable courses with actionable career tools and personalized guidance
Experience	**Transformation**	**Stakes**	**Positive future**
Choose a career track, follow self-paced courses, and gain tools like resume reviews, certifications, and mentorship to achieve your goals	Transition from uncertain and anxious to empowered, capable, and career-ready	Without this solution, the user risks being left behind in a competitive job market, missing out on opportunities to grow or pivot	Imagine having the confidence and skills to pursue your dream role, supported by a network of guidance and tools to make it happen

Do I recognize myself in this offer?
Am I comfortable to continues my exploration?
Yes, I continue
No, I give up

Can I continue with them?
Do I trust them respect them?
Do I clearly understand what they offer?
Yes, I continue
No, I give up

Am I excited with the proposed ture?
the experience engaging?
oes it relieve my pains?
es, I continue
o, I give up

©2024

Girls in Tech Empowerment Initiative *(P. 258)*

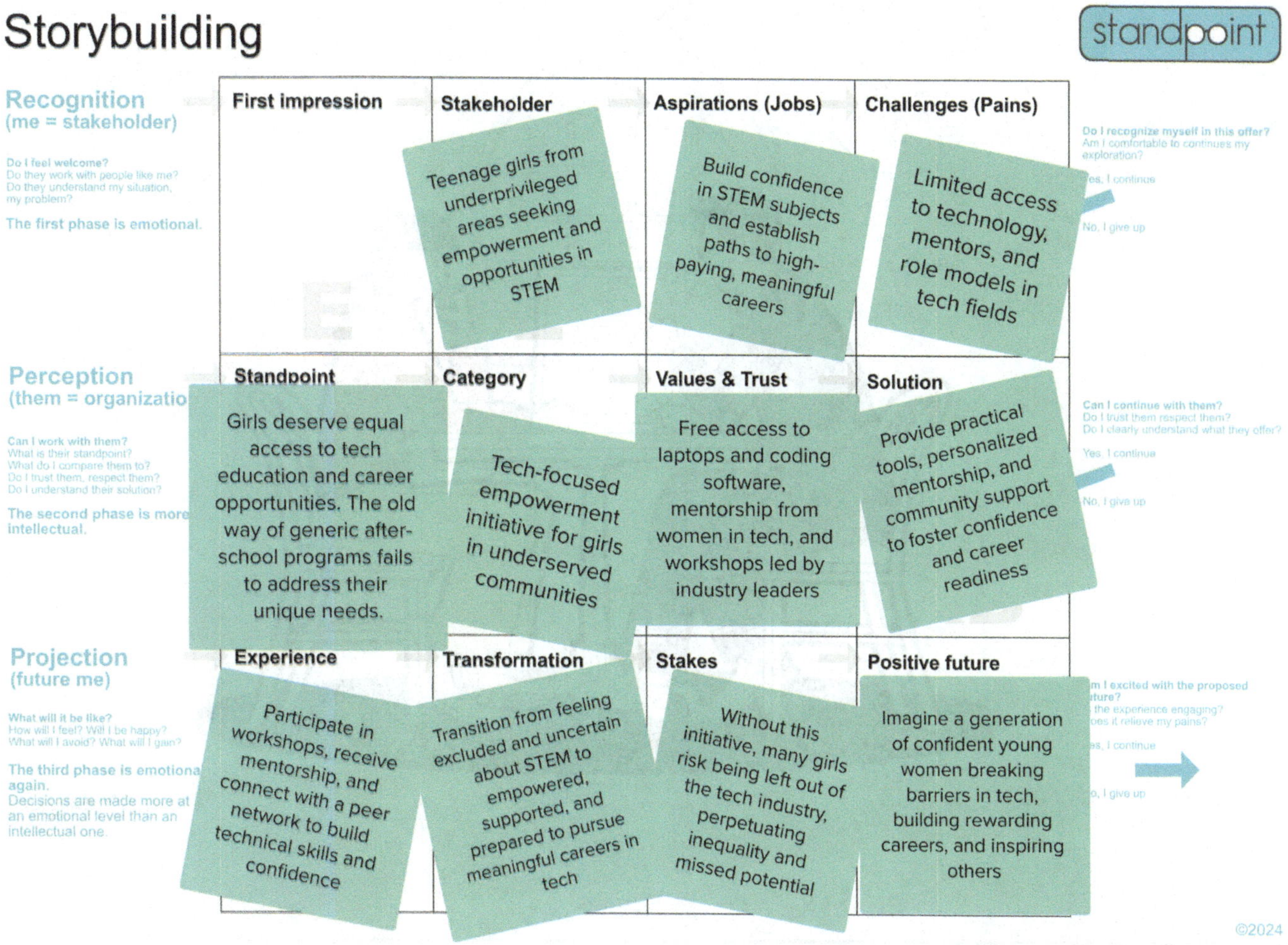

Storybuilding

TEST IF IT'S THE RIGHT STORY

12

Confront the world with your story, first by comparing to competing stories.

So, you've crafted your story. You've followed the framework, made smart decisions, and maybe even had a few "Aha!" moments along the way. But here's the real test: **Does it actually work?**

Before you print it on banners, slap it on your website, and start tattooing it on your sales team, let's run it through some **real-world testing**.

WHAT DOES YOUR TEAM THINK?

If you've been working with a broad group of colleagues throughout this process, congratulations! You've already had built-in critics (*ahem,* I mean, helpful reviewers).

Now, **widen the circle**:

- Run your story by team members who weren't involved in crafting it.
- Find a few fresh eyes—people who can act as stand-ins for your actual customers.
- Brace yourself for feedback (and maybe a few "But what does this actually mean?" moments).

The goal here isn't to destroy everything you've built—it's to **catch weak spots before they reach your audience**.

HOW DOES IT COMPARE TO COMPETITORS?

Let's be honest: **You're not the only one telling a story**. Your competitors are out there, trying to win the same audience. Time to put your story side-by-side with theirs and see if it stands out.

Ask yourself:

- **Who are they targeting?** (Is it the same people you're after?)
- **Are they clear?** (Or do they drown people in corporate jargon?)
- **What do they promise?** (And are they making bolder claims than you?)
- **Do they highlight aspirations and challenges?** (Or do they just list features?)
- **Do they have a different standpoint, a unique point of view?** (Or are they blending into the noise?)
- **Is their offer clearer than yours?** (Be honest. If it is, fix it.)
- **How do they present how it "happens"** (Are they simplifying the experience, or making it sound like rocket science?)

This isn't about copying—it's about **positioning**. You don't need to be louder than your competitors. You need to be **clearer, sharper, and more relevant**.

DOES IT FEEL RIGHT TO YOU?

Let's step back for a second. You've spent all this time crafting your story, but… **do YOU like it**?

Ask yourself:

- **Does it feel authentic?** (Or does it sound like a scripted ad?)
- **Would you be proud to share it?** (Or does it make you cringe?)
- **If someone else told this story, would you believe them?** (Or does it feel like marketing fluff?)

Your story should **excite you**. If you're not feeling it, your customers won't either.

IS IT SPARKING INTEREST?

Testing isn't about reading your story in a vacuum—it's about seeing how people react to it **in the wild**.

Try this:

- Share it in a casual conversation. Does the listener lean in or check their phone?
- Pitch it informally to a customer or prospect. Do they nod along or squint in confusion?
- Post a snippet on social media. Does it get engagement, or is it met with digital crickets?

The best test? **Does your story make people ask for more?**

If they respond with:

- "Wait, tell me more about that…" → You're onto something.
- "Cool." (followed by silence) → You've got work to do.

THE VERDICT: IS IT READY?

If you've tested your story, compared it to competitors, and gotten feedback (without having an existential crisis), you're in a great spot.

If something still feels off, **don't panic**. Storybuilding is an iterative process. Tweak, refine, and **don't be afraid to make bold changes**.

Remember: **A great story isn't just well-structured—it makes people feel something.**

Now, go put it to the test. And if all else fails, ask yourself:
"Would I bet my next vacation on this story working?"
If the answer is yes—you're good to go. If not? Time for a little more tweaking.

You will do this all again after crafting the story in chapter 13 (P. 191).

SIDE QUEST: YOUR COMPETITORS' POSITIONING C

So, you've got your story. It's solid. It's compelling. It's ready to take over the world. But before you crown yourself the category king (or queen), let's do a **quick reality check**: How does your story compare to the competition?

No, this isn't about copying them. It's about **understanding where you fit in** and making sure you're not just blending into the background like yet another beige website with "innovative solutions" in the tagline.

Here's a **quick and dirty** way to map out your competitors' positioning—without spending months in research reports or hiring a private investigator.

COMPETITOR HIT LIST

Start with a **list of your top competitors** - the ones your customers are also considering. If you don't know who they are (really?), Google your industry and see who shows up (or just ask your customers who else they looked at before choosing you).

Stalk Their Websites (In a Professional Way, Of Course)

Visit each competitor's homepage and ask yourself:

- What's their tagline? (Is it clear, or does it sound like corporate poetry?)
- How do they describe their positioning? (Are they the budget option? The premium choice? The "disruptor" who's actually been around for 20 years?)
- What themes do they highlight? (Are they all about efficiency, innovation, trust, sustainability?)
- Who are they targeting? (Is it the same audience as you, or are they going after a slightly different niche?)
- Is their messaging crystal clear, or do you need a PhD in Marketing to understand it?

Compare and Contrast (a.k.a. Spot the Copy-Paste Brands)

Now, step back and look at your notes. Do they all sound **exactly the same**? *(Spoiler: they might.)*

This is your opportunity to **stand out**. If every competitor is saying, "We help businesses grow," that's your cue to say something bold, specific, or—dare I say—interesting.

- Do they all position themselves as *cutting-edge*? Maybe your advantage is being *simple and no-nonsense.*
- Are they all *"customer-first"*? *(What a shocker!)* Maybe your strength is being results-driven instead.
- Are they vague about how their service works? Maybe you win by being refreshingly transparent.

Adjust Your Story (But Stay True to Yourself)

Now that you know how your competitors are positioning themselves, refine your own story:

Don't just be different for the sake of it (*"We're the only marketing agency run entirely by trained parrots!"*).

Do emphasize your real strengths in a way that customers actually care about.

Ask yourself:

- What do we offer that nobody else does?
- What's a pain point competitors ignore that we solve?
- If a customer was comparing options, what's our strongest argument for choosing us?

If needed, go back to B. Side Quest: Your Category on P. 141.

Final Thought: Own Your Space

You don't have to be the best at everything—you just have to be **the obvious choice for the right people**.

If your competitors are all playing it safe, take a stand. If they're all making vague promises, be specific. If they're all shouting, whisper (*metaphorically*—please don't literally whisper your tagline, that'd be weird).

The goal is **not** to fit in—it's to **stand out so much that customers can't ignore you**. Now, go own your space.

Competitors canvas

Competitors

standpoint

	Name	Tagline	Positioning	Themes	Target customers	Remarks
1						
2						
3						
4						
5						
YOU						

©2024

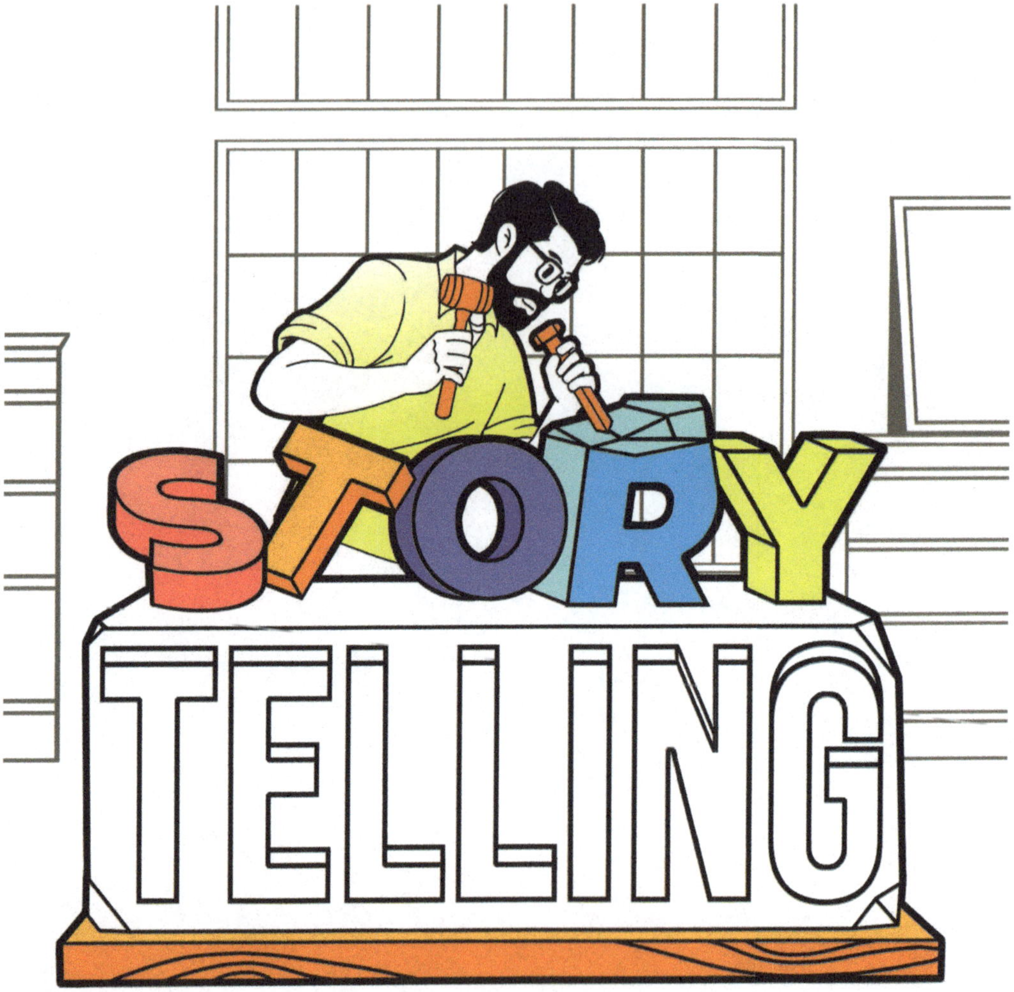
STORY
TELLING

THE STORY

13

You have the sequence, time to make it into a story.

Alright, you've done the groundwork. You've identified your customer's aspirations, pinpointed their challenges, and mapped out the key beats of your story. Now comes the moment of truth: turning this raw material into a compelling, structured narrative that actually *works.*

The good news? You don't have to be a literary genius or the next Shakespeare. You just need a clear structure, a bit of common sense, and a sprinkle of storytelling magic. Let's break it down.

JUST WRITE THE DAMN THING

First things first: don't overthink it. Too many people freeze up when they start writing, agonizing over the perfect words. Here's the trick—just start. Get the basic structure down, and you can refine later.

Think of it like making a sandwich. You start with the bread (your core message), then layer in the fillings (details that bring it to life), and finally add the sauce (emotion, humor, or anything that makes it memorable). Never forget that without the bread, even the best sandwich just falls apart.

So, step one: slap down the main elements.

Later, you'll tailor it for different formats:

- A short "networking introduction" (a.k.a. the "So, what do you do?" moment)
- A full website narrative
- A pitch for investors, customers, or partners
- A sales script that doesn't sound robotic
- A snappy video script
- Anything else where words matter (spoiler: that's everywhere)

Start long, then trim it down as needed. It's always easier to cut than to add.

The first column (bold black) is a call back to the squares of the previous canvas.

On each line, put a short sentence.

- The first column in blue contains the core elements. You can use just these for a short story. The elevator pitch. Just the essentials.
- The second blue column adds depth. More detail, for when you have a captive audience.
- And the third is the full Monty. The whole narrative, used for things like websites or big presentations.

This gives you three lengths of story to start using right away.

THE SHORTEST

For example, at an event, if someone asks what you do.

- These people / this type of company has this aspiration but/or this challenge
- Our solution is xxx
- This is why their life is better

Which is better?

- I mow lawns.

Or

- People are ashamed of their messy lawns, but are too tired after work to take care of them.
- I mow their lawn.
- They are proud of their yard in front of their neighbors.

THE STORY ELEMENTS

First impression

Brand Persona. Blurb / tagline.

This is here to be sure you keep it top of mind while writing the others.

Stakeholder (Customer)

This type of person / company...

Describe your ideal client so that they recognize themselves.

Aspirations (Jobs)

Has this aspiration...

Your chosen important choice of aspiration.

Challenges (Pains)

But, there is a problem...

Your chosen important choice of challenge.

Standpoint

Old way vs new way...

A strong differentiator.

Category

In this new category...

What you want them to compare you to.

Values & Trust

You can trust us because...

Short list of trust signals. To be extended on your homepage for example.

Solution

Here is our solution...

A clear presentation of your offer.

Experience

There is a simple 3 steps process...

Or salient steps in the customer journey. They need to visualize it.

Transformation

You will become...

This is great if you can make it work

Stakes

You will avoid...

A list of problems that you solve (but didn't make the top spot).

Positive future

Your life will be better...

A list of positive outcomes that you deliver (but didn't make the top spot).

Easy interaction

Simple Call-to-action.

COMBINATIONS

It's important and useful to create separate phrases for each step as a first draft. It clarifies your ideas.

Often it will end up being more subtle.

For example, the aspiration or the challenge can actually be the factor that defines your customer.

For example:

- Caring young parents: "caring" is the aspiration.
- Struggling young parents: "struggling" is the problem.

CONSISTENCY

You need to have **one** story.

If you need to tell a different story to an investor than to your customers, something is up. Who are you lying to?

For your marketplace, if you tell a different story to buyers and sellers, they will know!

Of course, you will have **variations** of your core story for different stakeholders.

The Story

standpoint

Storybuilding canvas

Recognition	First impression	Emotional
	Stakeholder	
	Aspirations (Jobs)	
	Challenges (Pains)	
Perception	Standpoint	Intellectual
	Category	
	Values & Trust	
	Solution	
Projection	Experience	Emotional
	Transformation	
	Stakes	
	Positive future	
	Easy interaction	

COPYWRITING

The depth of your copywriting is entirely up to you—like deciding whether to dip your toes in the pool or cannonball into the deep end.

Start with the basics - a simple sequence of sentences.

Then, refine by combining steps and improving the flow (think of it as upgrading from a grocery list to a poetic love letter about your favorite snacks).

Finally, craft a complete, cohesive narrative and practice reading it aloud. This last step is crucial—it helps you determine whether your words roll off the tongue like a smooth jazz solo or trip over themselves like a toddler in oversized shoes. Either way, practice makes perfect (or at least entertaining)!

FACING THE REAL WORLD (BRACE YOURSELF!)

Alright, time to leave the cozy world of brainstorming and see if your story survives in the wild. Ideally, you've got some happy clients—real people, not just the ones in your head—who can act as sounding boards.

Tell them you're not fishing for compliments (even though a little ego boost never hurts), but genuinely want their feedback. Then hit them with these questions:

- Do they recognize themselves and their situation? Was that engaging?
- What benefits will they receive?
- What challenges or problems do you help them alleviate?
- How are you different? What would they compare you to?
- Do they understand how things will happen? Are they comfortable with that?
- Do they imagine positive outcomes?

Now, take a deep breath. Are you still in love with your story, or does it need a little more work? Either way, you're one step closer to crafting something truly compelling!

EXAMPLES

Part 5—on P. 209—presents a number of full examples of the four steps of Storybuilding.

Here are three examples of the Story canvas to give you an idea.

Non-Profit: Sustainable Urban Living and Community Wellness
(P. 254)

Storybuilding

Stage	Element	Content	Appeal
Recognition	First impression		Emotional
	Stakeholder	You're an urban resident living without personal green space, longing for fresh, organic produce and meaningful connections in your community.	
	Aspirations (Jobs)	You aspire to grow your own food, foster a sense of belonging, and contribute to eco-friendly practices.	
	Challenges (Pains)	But the challenges of limited access to affordable produce, isolation, and a lack of gardening knowledge make these goals feel unattainable.	
Perception	Standpoint	Everyone deserves the opportunity to grow their own food, connect with neighbors, and live more sustainably, no matter where they live.	Intellectual
	Category	That's why we created an urban community garden initiative focused on making gardening accessible and collaborative for all.	
	Values & Trust	We provide centralized garden plots, free-to-use tools, seeds, and educational workshops to empower urban residents.	
	Solution	By addressing food insecurity and fostering community networks, we help participants grow fresh produce while building lifelong skills.	
Projection	Experience	Start by securing your garden plot, accessing tools and seeds, and learning sustainable practices through workshops.	Emotional
	Transformation	Imagine connecting with like-minded neighbors, celebrating harvest festivals, and sharing surplus produce with those in need.	
	Stakes	Without this initiative, urban residents may remain disconnected from their food sources and their community.	
	Positive future	Now imagine a thriving urban space where gardens bloom, friendships flourish, and sustainability becomes a way of life.	
	Easy interaction		

Storybuilding

standpoint

Phase	Element	Content	Appeal
Recognition	First impression.		Emotional
Recognition	Stakeholder	You're a high-net-worth individual or venture capitalist seeking groundbreaking investment opportunities in deep tech.	Emotional
Recognition	Aspirations (Jobs)	You aspire to achieve outsized financial returns, support innovative global solutions, and position yourself as a visionary in cutting-edge technology.	Emotional
Recognition	Challenges (Pains)	Yet, the complexity of emerging technologies, long ROI timelines, and competition make this space challenging to navigate.	Emotional
Perception	Standpoint	Investing in deep tech should balance bold ambition with informed decision-making, empowering you to lead in high-stakes innovation.	Intellectual
Perception	Category	That's why we've developed a deep tech startup that connects investors to transformative technologies through clear insights and a well-defined strategy.	Intellectual
Perception	Values & Trust	With a multidisciplinary team, robust business cases, and exclusive partnerships, we ensure both credibility and first-mover advantage.	Intellectual
Perception	Solution	Our approach includes simplifying complex ideas, offering unique engagement opportunities, and providing detailed roadmaps for product and market success.	Intellectual
Projection	Experience	Through clear explanations, real-time updates, and access to exclusive events, you'll feel informed and connected throughout your investment journey.	Emotional
Projection	Transformation	Picture yourself as a key backer of innovations solving global challenges, celebrated for supporting transformative technologies.	Emotional
Projection	Stakes	Without this opportunity, you risk missing high-impact investments and losing competitive edge in the deep tech arena.	Emotional
Projection	Positive future	Now imagine building a future-proof portfolio, advancing global innovation, and achieving outsized financial and societal returns.	Emotional
Projection	Easy interaction		Emotional

Investor: Deep Tech Startup Looking for Funding *(P. 272)*

Non-Profit: Wildlife Rescue and Rehabilitation (P. 259)

Storybuilding

standpoint

Recognition	**First impression**		Emotional
	Stakeholder	You're a nature lover who cares deeply about protecting wildlife and preserving biodiversity but often feels unsure of how to help.	
	Aspirations (Jobs)	You aspire to safeguard endangered species and make a meaningful contribution to conservation efforts.	
	Challenges (Pains)	Yet, limited knowledge, time, and financial constraints make it difficult to take direct action, leaving you feeling helpless.	
Perception	**Standpoint**	Conservation should be accessible, impactful, and locally driven, connecting people to tangible outcomes that make a difference.	Intellectual
	Category	That's why we created Wildlife Rescue and Rehabilitation, a community-focused initiative dedicated to rescuing and protecting wildlife.	
	Values & Trust	Our 24/7 rescue hotline and free medical care services ensure injured animals receive immediate and professional attention.	
	Solution	Through educational programs and hands-on volunteer opportunities, we empower individuals to actively engage in conservation efforts.	
Projection	**Experience**	Call our 24/7 hotline to report injured wildlife, participate in rehabilitation efforts, and attend wildlife release events to witness the results of your contributions.	Emotional
	Transformation	Imagine celebrating the recovery and release of rehabilitated animals, knowing your actions directly impacted their survival.	
	Stakes	Without this initiative, countless injured animals may go without care, and nature lovers miss opportunities to contribute meaningfully.	
	Positive future	Now picture a future where you're part of a thriving community of conservationists, helping to preserve local biodiversity and foster a deeper connection with nature.	
	Easy interaction		

SIDE QUEST: YOUR TAGLINE

D

Let's talk about taglines—the tiny but mighty one-liner that sums up your brand's essence. A tagline is like your brand's elevator pitch but compressed into a bite-sized nugget of brilliance. It's the thing that sticks in people's heads long after they've scrolled past your website or walked away from your pitch.

A great tagline does more than sound good; it works hard. It communicates your unique benefit, mission, or perspective in six or seven words (because let's be honest, no one remembers long-winded taglines).

The Golden Rules of Taglines

1. **Keep it short.** More than seven words, and it starts to lose punch.
2. **Make it memorable.** If people repeat it back to you, you've nailed it.
3. **Be unique.** If your competitor can use it too, it's not special enough.
4. **Communicate a benefit.** "We're the best" isn't a benefit. "We make Mondays suck less" is.
5. **Avoid corporate jargon.** Nobody dreams of "leveraging scalable solutions."
6. **Bonus points for humor.** If it makes people smile, they'll remember it.

The Tagline Test

Think you've got a good one? Run it through these questions:

- Can someone read it once and remember it?
- Would it make sense on a T-shirt or sticker?
- If you swap out your brand name for a competitor's, does it still work? (If yes, rewrite it.)
- Does it trigger curiosity or a reaction?

Tagline Inspiration: The Cheat Sheet

If you're stuck, here are some patterns to play with:

- **Problem-Solution:** "No More Bad Coffee. Ever."
- **Unexpected Twist:** "Boring Meetings? Not on Our Watch."
- **Category Redefiner: "**Not Just Another To-Do App."
- **Challenge the Status Quo:** "Because Banking Shouldn't Suck."
- **Aspirational:** "Helping You Win at Adulting."
- **Benefit-Driven:** "Faster, Simpler, Better Marketing."

Pro Tip: Be Brutally Honest

Before settling on a tagline, be brutally honest with yourself. If your tagline sounds generic, rewrite it. If it feels forced, loosen it up. If it doesn't excite *you*, it won't excite anyone else.

Now, go forth and craft something unforgettable. Your tagline deserves better than mediocrity.

Books

If you want to delve further into **taglines**.

Taglines

A Few Storybuilding tagline ideas

- Your brand from their standpoint
- Low engagement, Storybuild your brand
- You talk about you, they yawn
- Taking their standpoint is engaging
- Talk about them, they will think of you
- Stop talking about you

ASK AI TAGLINES

Your company:

- Suggest taglines that convey the value proposition and uniqueness in a short, memorable, clever way.

Ask your favorite AI chat bot.

Get the prompt. Copy, paste, adapt and run.

Get the Prompt

PART 5:
HOW YOU WILL USE IT

Your story isn't one-size-fits-all—it adapts. Whether for different audiences, channels, or business cases, Storybuilding flexes to fit. In this section, we'll explore how to apply it effectively and see it in action.

NGO
STORYBUILDING
APPLICATIONS

WHAT AND WHERE 14

Let's explore…

Variations

Variations

You can build a story for

- Your company
- A department
- A product or service range
- A specific product or service
- A specific campaign
- A project

Apply the same sequence, shifting the focus to the specific level needed.

There will, of course, be some overlap between your different stories.

Channels

Channels

Use your story everywhere.

Website

Your website is a core foundation of your brand.

Your customer's experience can determine their trust and interest.

Of all the applications, your website allows for extensive options to present your story.

Information can be displayed as text, images, video, or a combination of them.

It can be of any length as long as it remains engaging.

It is a good first application. Starting with the longest, most extensive version makes it easier to create shorter, simplified ones.

Sales Pitch

One of these shorter versions is the sales pitch.

Customers love hearing you talk about them. Tell *their* story.

Customers love hearing you talk about them.

Investor Pitch

A story that engages your customers will boost sales.

Presenting that same story to investors shows them that you have a convincing narrative for your go-to-market strategy.

Even a boring IT mini-project list

Every big company has a long list of must-do IT mini-projects such as "Upgrade server 12 to latest security patch level". Going through such a list with management is like pulling teeth. And the person responsible gets no recognition.

You can convey the importance of these tasks using a short version of Storybuilding. For each project add a few fields to the spreadsheet:

- Impacted audience (e.g. the company)
- Problem (e.g. risk of being hacked)
- Solution (e.g. patch)
- Why their life will be better (e.g. reputation safe)

It can be used *everywhere.*

Contrast your own brands

Usually, you choose to work on your overall company, a product range or a specific product. One special case is when you have several "brands" with similar products.

There will be significant overlap in many aspects of your value proposition: target segments, aspirations, challenges, standpoint, category, experience, benefits.

To contrast these different brands, you will need to select different angles to concentrate on.

In this case, it will be important to work through them in parallel, choosing which element is best for each "brand" as you go along. This will help create contrasting stories.

A few simplistic examples:

Compare with your competors' stories

Your story doesn't exist in a vacuum—it competes for attention, trust, and relevance. Customers are constantly comparing your brand's narrative to others, whether consciously or not. That's why understanding your competitors' stories is essential. If their message is similar, you risk blending in; if it's drastically different, you need to position yourself in a way that makes your story the obvious choice.

Differentiation isn't just about what you offer—it's about how you frame it. The right story not only sets you apart but also reshapes the conversation in your favor.

TYPES OF APPLICATION 15

Pretty much anywhere

B2C – Business to Consumer

- Subscription Boxes for Self-Care and Wellness
- Indoor Gardening Kits for Small Spaces
- Online Skills Training and Career Development Platform

B2B – Business to Business

- IT Support for Co-Working Spaces
- Sustainable Office Supplies for Small Businesses

Non-profit

- Urban Community Garden Initiative
- Girls in Tech Empowerment Initiative
- Wildlife Rescue and Rehabilitation

Marketplace

- Handmade Art & Craft Marketplace
- Peer-to-Peer Rental Marketplace

Differentiating competing stories

- Small B2C Coffee Shops

Investor

- Deep tech startup looking for funding

Internal project pitch

- A Product Manager Pitching a New Productivity App for Remote Teams

SIDE QUEST: YOUR OFFER

E

OFFERS: GOOD, BETTER, BEST

If you offer services, having a three-tiered offering instead of a single offer provides significant strategic advantages for businesses, catering to diverse customer needs and maximizing revenue opportunities.

Appeals to a Broader Audience

With three tiers—typically categorized as basic, standard, and premium—you can address varying budget levels and priorities. Customers who are price-sensitive can opt for the basic tier, while those seeking advanced features or added value can choose the premium option.

Encourages Upselling and Increased Revenue:

A tiered approach creates opportunities for upselling. The standard tier often serves as the anchor, showing the value customers receive at a reasonable price. Meanwhile, the premium tier demonstrates enhanced features, enticing customers to upgrade for the "best" experience. This structure often leads to higher average revenue per customer.

Helps Customers Make Decisions:

Offering a single option can leave customers feeling unsure about its value. Three tiers, with clear distinctions, guide decision-making and create a sense of choice. "Which should I buy?" instead of "Should I buy?" Behavioral psychology suggests that people often select the middle tier, perceiving it as the most balanced option.

Differentiates Value:

With three tiers, you can highlight what makes each level unique, showcasing your ability to meet a range of needs without alienating any segment of your market. This approach boosts customer satisfaction and retention.

What is the best way to structure your three tiers?

They should be based on how we perceive value. There are four levers you can use to differentiate value: Certainty, Time to Value, Effort and Exclusivity.

VALUE PERCEPTION LEVERS

Certainty

If people are certain they will receive the promised value, they will pay a high price. If they doubt, their propensity to pay diminishes in proportion to the doubt. Enhance their sense of certainty.

Enhance their sense of certainty.

I have a gym membership. I doubt I will receive the promised value (getting fit). Because I don't go often enough. If I chose to have a private coach, it would dramatically increase my certainty of success. People pay 5 or 10 times more for lifting the same weights and running on the same treadmills because they then more strongly believe they will succeed (receive the promised value).

Are your customers certain that they will receive the promised value?

What makes people doubt?

How can you increase their sense of certainty?

Time to value

If I will receive the promised value immediately, I am willing to pay more than if I have to wait. For some luxury vehicles, a (recent) used one available immediately is more expensive than the new one with a long waiting time.

How much time until they receive the promised value?

How can you shorten the actual time or the perceived time to value?

Structured timeline, defined milestones, early benefits & AHA moments, ...

Effort

If there is little effort to receive the promised value, I will pay more than if it will be hard.

Ikea furniture, where you build it yourself, is cheaper than traditional brands.

How much effort is there for your customers?

How can you reduce the effort needed?

Simplified onboarding and/or migration, automation, templates, standard configurations, ...

The fourth one is a little different.

Exclusivity

Scarcity and exclusivity drive prices up.

The private club, the limited edition, the unique artwork…

How exclusive is your offer?

Can anyone easily receive the value?

What could make your offer feel like a commodity?

How can you increase the sense of exclusivity?

Limited "seats", strict application process, personalization, high price, extra perks, limited access, ...

Offers: Good, Better, Best canvas

Offers: Good, Better, Best

standpoint

Certainty

1

Exclusivity

2

Time, Effort & Cost to the organisation

High Effort ↑

Stakeholder's standpoint

Time to value

3

Effort

4

5

Low Effort ↓

Good	**Better**	**Best**
6	7	8

©2024

LET'S BUILD YOUR 3-TIER OFFER

Time, Effort & Cost To The Organization

From the organization's standpoint, the idea will be structuring their offers so that

- the lower tier is highly scalable, requiring little effort and resources on their part
- the middle tier requires more effort or resources
- the top tier can be labor intensive or require extra resources

Think:

- Do-It-Yourself
- Do it with you
- Do it for you

How much does delivering value cost your organization in time, effort, and money?

Which parts "cost" you the most? Which are "free"?

How can you reduce those costs to increase scalability?

What could you build to offer similar value but with less cost to your organization?

For example, digital products, which, once created, require no additional cost, such as online courses, books, graphic assets, or other resources...

In addition, high-appeal/low-cost features are often less about the actual product and more about the customer experience.

GOOD, BETTER, BEST

Rafi Mohammed wrote an interesting article in the Harvard Business Review.

Good, Better, Best

Good

How can you bundle your value to be low "cost," so very scalable, with a potentially low price? There might be an upfront cost to produce all or parts of the offer in this form, but the incremental cost will be meager. This Good offer will probably require time and effort from your customers, reducing their certainty that they will receive the promised value. Since it will be widely available, there will be a low sense of exclusivity.

Book, video, online course, simplified, automated or template-based solutions...

Better

How can you bundle your products and services for a Better offer that requires less time and effort and that increases the customer's confidence in receiving the promised value?

This is often your initial or standard offer. Too much or too expensive for some, who will go for the Good offer. Others will want more, with cost being less of an issue, and will go for the Best offer.

Best

How can you bundle your value to deliver the most value to your customers?

How can you reduce the required time and effort even more, and dramatically increase the certainty of value?

How can you make your offer very exclusive? Limited "seats," the strict application process, high price, extra perks, limited access...

What could you add to deliver more value, improve the experience, and be the Best offer?

For example, this can be a high-end, very hands-on, do-it-for-you service.

To ensure sharp distinctions between offerings, no more than four attributes should differ between Good and Better and between Better and Best.

The canvas will identify the four levers applicable to your offers, will help you classify your features based on the cost to your company. This will allow to bundle your offer in three tiers: Good, Better and Best.

ASK AI GOOD, BETTER, BEST

Your company:

- Create a three-tiered offer based on three ways people perceive value: certainty of receiving the promised value, time and effort needed to receive that value.

Ask your favorite AI chat bot.

Get the Prompt ◀ ***Get the prompt.*** Copy, paste, adapt and run.

NEW
PURCHASE ONLINE
$9.9
SCAN TO BUY

B2C-BUSINESS TO CONSUMER

16

The most obvious usage is for B2C companies.

B2C companies live and die by their ability to connect with individual customers. And the best ones? They don't just sell a product—they make you *feel* something. Whether it's excitement, trust, or the unshakable belief that you *need* another houseplant, great brands know how to tell a story that sticks.

In this chapter, we're bringing the Storybuilding method to life with real-world examples—showing you how brands take storytelling from theory to practice. Think of this as your creative spark, not a rulebook. The goal isn't to box you in but to open up new ways of thinking about how your brand can speak to your customers' needs, emotions, and wildest aspirations.

So, let's dive in and see how the right story can turn casual shoppers into raving fans—the kind who don't just buy from you, but *swear by* you.

B2C – Business to Consumer

- Subscription Boxes for Self-Care and Wellness
- Indoor Gardening Kits for Small Spaces
- Online Skills Training and Career Development Platform

Subscription Boxes for Self-Care and Wellness

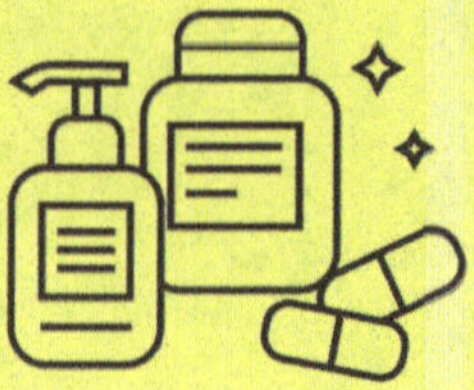

Stakeholder (customer)

standpoint

Scope

- Subscription Boxes for Self-Care and Wellness

Segments

- Busy professionals, primarily women, interested in wellness and self-care

Aspiration (Jobs)

- Feel relaxed, rejuvenated, and cared for
- Enhance their lifestyle
- Feel at their best

Challenges (Pains)

- Incorporate self-care into their routine despite a busy schedule
- Lack of time to research and buy wellness products
- Feeling overwhelmed by stress and burnout
- Uncertainty about which products are truly effective or worth the money

Extras

- They value authenticity, high quality, and ethical sourcing
- They want to feel pampered and empowered, with minimal effort
- They prioritize brands that are eco-conscious and socially responsible

Triggers

- Experiencing a particularly stressful week or burnout
- Starting a new job or life transition that demands more self-care
- Searching for a thoughtful gift for themselves or a friend

Current Solution

- Buying random self-care products from stores or online retailers
- Following recommendations from friends or influencers without consistency

Importance

©2024

Organization (company)

standpoint

Enablers

- A selection of premium self-care items, such as candles, skincare, bath salts, and mindfulness tools
- Ability to personalize boxes based on preferences or needs (e.g., stress relief, energy boost)
- Guides and tips included in each box for maximizing the benefits of the products

Solvers

- Auto-delivery of monthly boxes saves customers time and effort
- Partnering with wellness experts to vet products ensures quality and effectiveness
- Biodegradable and sustainable materials to ease eco-conscious concerns

Experience

- The subscription model ensures seamless delivery
- Ability to personalize their boxes based on their needs, such as stress relief or energy boosts
- The surprise bonus item in every box and the occasional self-care challenges
- Exclusive access to forums or apps allows them to share experiences and tips

Uniqueness

- Focuses on both physical and mental well-being, blending mindfulness tools with skincare and wellness products
- Prioritizes ethical and sustainable sourcing for all products
- Offers a "pause anytime" subscription option to reduce commitment anxiety

Brand Persona

- Warm, nurturing, and empowering - a "best friend" who helps you prioritize yourself
- Tone emphasizes encouragement and positivity
- Modern yet cozy, using soft colors and clean design

Extra Delight

- A surprise "bonus item" in every box
- Monthly self-care challenges (e.g., "30 days of mindfulness")
- Access to a community forum: subscribers can connect, share tips, and learn

Matching

©2024

Subscription Boxes for Self-Care and Wellness

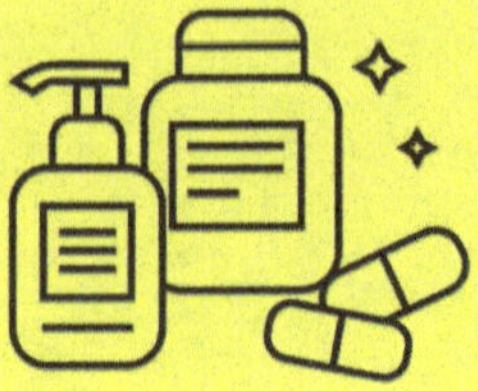

Storybuilding

standpoint

Recognition
(me = stakeholder)

Do I feel welcome?
Do they work with people like me?
Do they understand my situation, my problem?

The first phase is emotional.

First impression	Stakeholder	Aspirations (Jobs)	Challenges (Pains)
	Busy professionals, primarily women, juggling work, life, and wellness goals	Feel relaxed, rejuvenated, and cared for while enhancing their lifestyle and achieving their best self	Struggling to incorporate self-care into their routine due to lack of time and overwhelming product choices

Do I recognize myself in this offer?
Am I comfortable to continues my exploration?

Yes, I continue

No, I give up

Perception
(them = organizatio

Can I work with them?
What is their standpoint?
What do I compare them to?
Do I trust them, respect them?
Do I understand their solution?

The second phase is more intellectual.

Standpoint	Category	Values & Trust	Solution
Self-care should be easy and enjoyable. The old way of piecemeal solutions is inefficient; the new way is curated and seamless	Premium subscription boxes for holistic self-care	Products are ethically sourced, vetted by wellness experts, and delivered in eco-friendly packaging	Monthly delivery of personalized wellness products, educational guides, and surprise bonuses

Can I continue with them?
Do I trust them respect them?
Do I clearly understand what they offer?

Yes, I continue

No, I give up

Projection
(future me)

What will it be like?
How will I feel? Will I be happy?
What will I avoid? What will I gain?

The third phase is emotional again.
Decisions are made more at an emotional level than an intellectual one.

Experience	Transformation	Stakes	Positive future
Pick your theme, customize preferences, and receive a seamless delivery of curated self-care products	From feeling stressed and overlooked to feeling empowered, cared for, and at ease	Without this solution, stress and burnout may persist, and self-care remains a distant goal	Envision a life where self-care is a joyful, empowering habit that brings relaxation and energy to your everyday life

Am I excited with the proposed future?
Is the experience engaging?
Does it relieve my pains?

Yes, I continue

No, I give up

©2024

Storybuilding

standpoint

Stage	Element	Text	Mode
Recognition	**First impression**		Emotional
Recognition	**Stakeholder**	You're a busy professional juggling the demands of work, home, and life, longing for moments of relaxation and care that help you feel your best.	Emotional
Recognition	**Aspirations (Jobs)**	Imagine finally feeling pampered and rejuvenated, with your lifestyle enhanced by thoughtful, high-quality products.	Emotional
Recognition	**Challenges (Pains)**	Yet, finding the time to research and choose effective wellness items feels overwhelming, leaving you stuck in the cycle of stress and burnout.	Emotional
Perception	**Standpoint**	At our core, we believe self-care should be effortless and guilt-free, which is why we've reimagined wellness with our curated subscription boxes.	Intellectual
Perception	**Category**	Designed as premium solutions for holistic self-care, our boxes combine the best of skincare, mindfulness tools, and lifestyle enhancements.	Intellectual
Perception	**Values & Trust**	Every product is ethically sourced, expert-vetted, and eco-conscious, giving you peace of mind while nurturing your well-being.	Intellectual
Perception	**Solution**	With monthly deliveries of customizable self-care products and thoughtful guides, we take the guesswork out of creating a routine that works for you.	Intellectual
Projection	**Experience**	Getting started is simple: choose a theme, personalize your preferences, and enjoy seamless monthly deliveries that fit perfectly into your busy life.	Emotional
Projection	**Transformation**	Imagine transitioning from feeling stressed and neglected to empowered and rejuvenated, with every box bringing moments of joy and care.	Emotional
Projection	**Stakes**	Without a solution like this, stress and burnout will continue to take their toll, keeping self-care out of reach.	Emotional
Projection	**Positive future**	But now, envision a life where self-care is a joyful habit—where you feel energized, confident, and ready to take on life's challenges.	Emotional
Projection	**Easy interaction**		Emotional

Tagline ideas

- "Self-Care, Made Simple."
- "Relax, Rejuvenate, Repeat."
- "Effortless Wellness, Delivered."
- "Your Wellness, Your Way."

Indoor Gardening Kits for Small Space

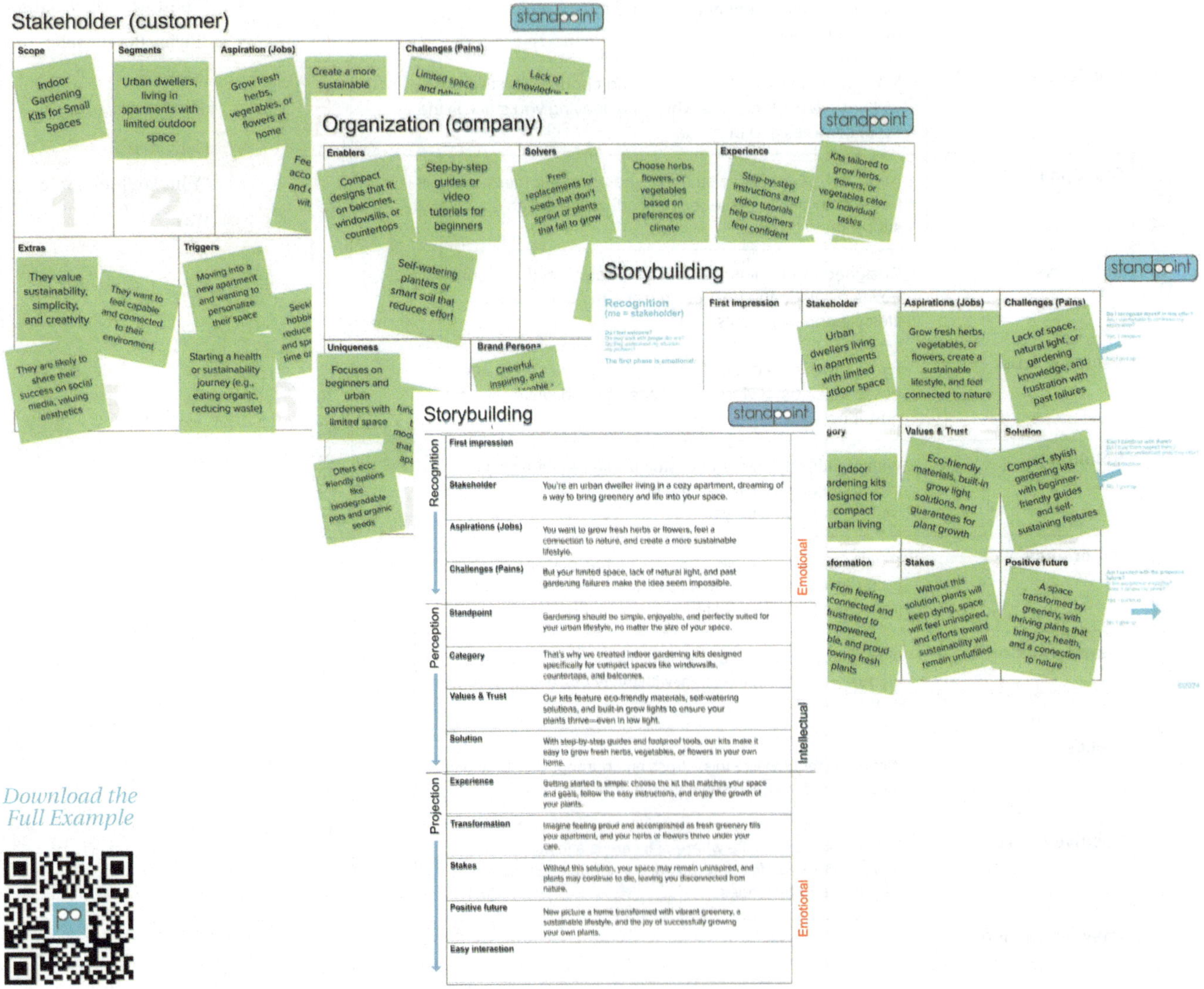

Download the Full Example

Online Skills Training and Career Development Platform

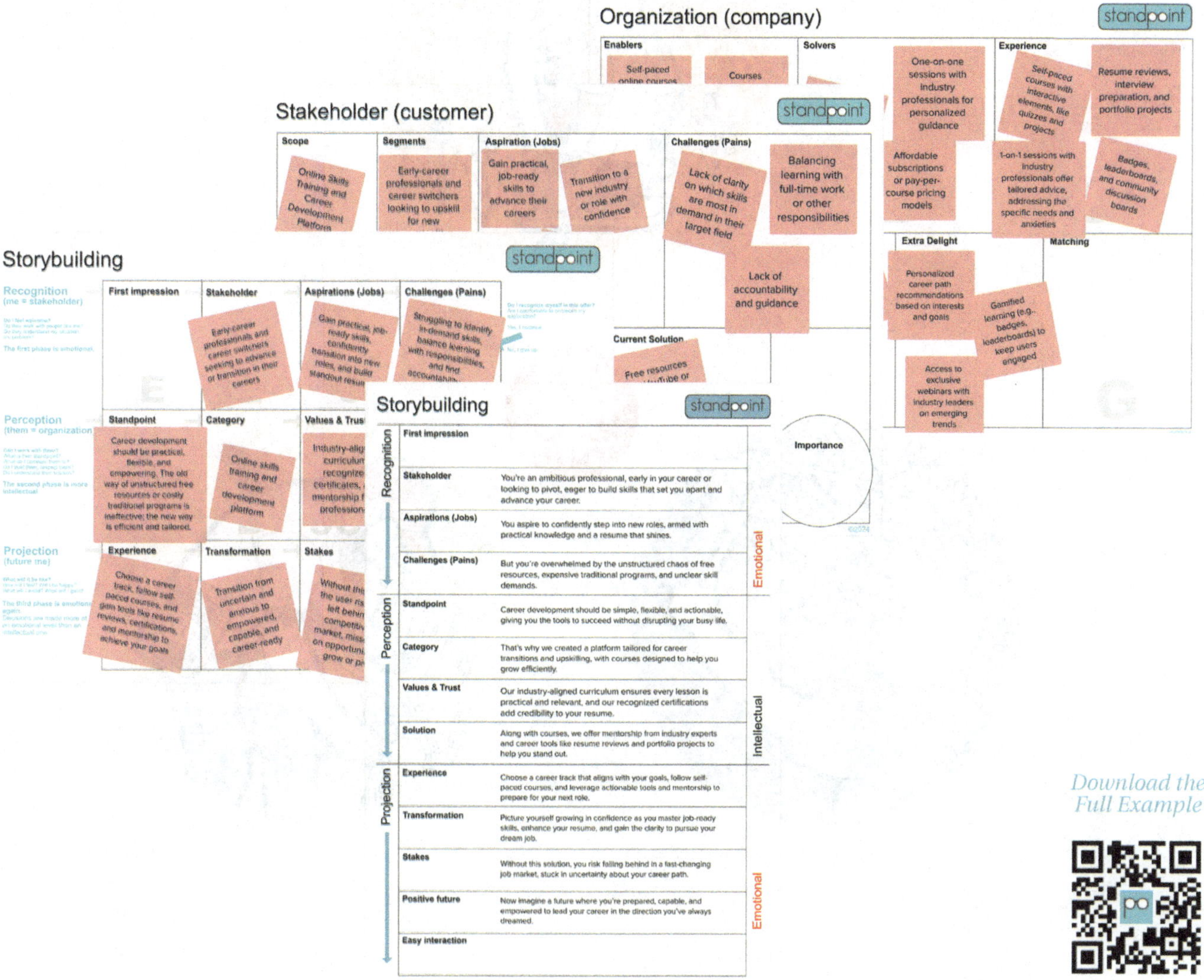

Download the Full Example

FELCO
SWISS MADE
FELCO

CASE STUDY: FELCO

17

The world leader in garden shears needed to contrast their three brands

BACKGROUND: A LEGACY OF EXCELLENCE

For over 80 years, FELCO has been synonymous with high-quality, durable tools designed for professionals. Known for their Swiss precision and repairability, FELCO tools have built a strong reputation among horticulturists, landscapers, arborists, and agricultural workers.

However, as the brand expanded its portfolio, new challenges emerged:

- How to clearly differentiate FELCO's core brand from new offerings.
- How to target distinct customer segments without diluting the FELCO identity.
- How to ensure distributors and retailers understood and communicated these differences effectively.

To address these challenges, FELCO adopted the **Storybuilding** method to craft distinct, customer-centric narratives for its three brands: **FELCO, FELCO Prosumer, and Alpen**.

THE CHALLENGE: CONFUSION IN THE MARKETPLACE

As FELCO evolved, two new brands emerged:

- **FELCO Prosumer:** A premium line designed for discerning "prosumers" who wanted professional-grade tools with a refined design.
- **Alpen:** A separate brand created to introduce rugged, motorized tools for adventurers and extreme conditions.

The risk was clear—without differentiation, these brands could either compete with each other or confuse potential customers. FELCO needed a compelling way to **position each brand** while maintaining a unified overarching identity.

THE SOLUTION: STORYBUILDING IN ACTION

Rather than focusing on **what FELCO makes**, Storybuilding shifted the perspective to **who FELCO serves**. Using the three core Storybuilding phases—**Recognition, Perception, and Projection**—the team crafted distinct brand narratives.

Recognition: Speaking to the Right Audience

Each brand was positioned to immediately resonate with its ideal customer:

- **FELCO:** "Trusted by Professionals" – Tools designed for horticulturists, landscapers, arborists, and agricultural workers seeking precision and longevity.
- **FELCO Prosumer:** "Luxury Meets Performance" – Tools for those who demand professional-grade quality while embracing personal style and ergonomic comfort.
- **Alpen:** "Master the Wild" – Power tools engineered for adventurers tackling extreme environments.

Perception: Aligning with Customer Values

To reinforce differentiation, each brand emphasized unique attributes:

- **FELCO:** Performance, Ergonomics, Durability.
- **FELCO Prosumer:** Pleasure, Comfort, Eco-responsibility—Style without sacrificing performance.
- **Alpen:** Overcoming physical limitations with lightweight yet powerful tools.

Projection: Crafting a Compelling Future for the Customer

A strong brand story should help customers **imagine themselves using the product**:

- **FELCO:** "Imagine the pride of using tools that enhance your craft and last a lifetime."
- **FELCO Prosumer:** "Envision tools that are an extension of your identity—luxury and precision in every cut."
- **Alpen:** "Picture yourself conquering nature's toughest challenges with confidence."

THE CANVASES

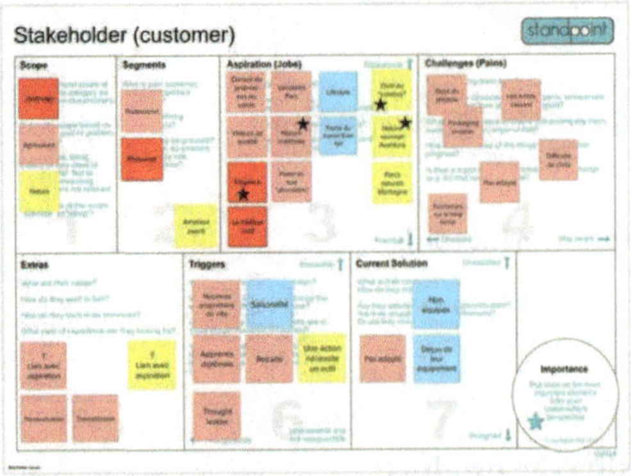

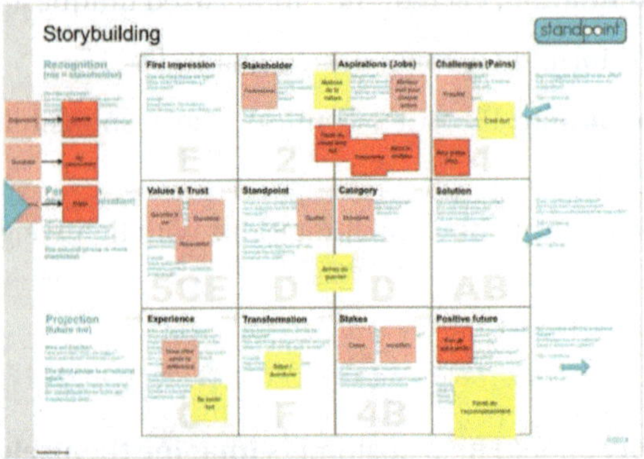

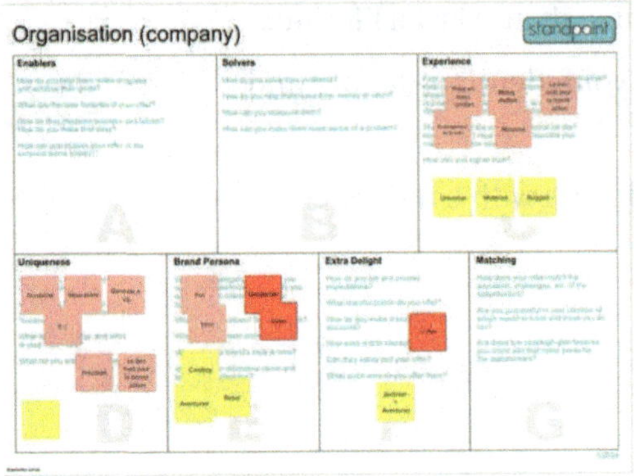

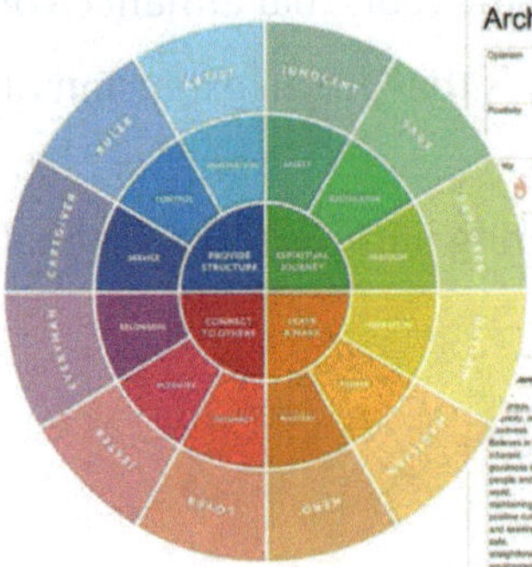

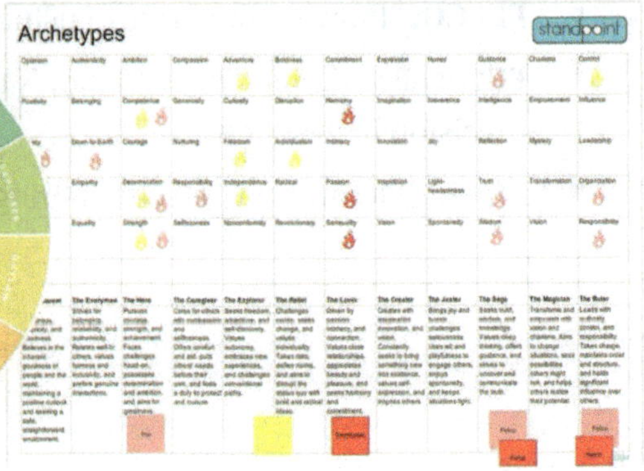

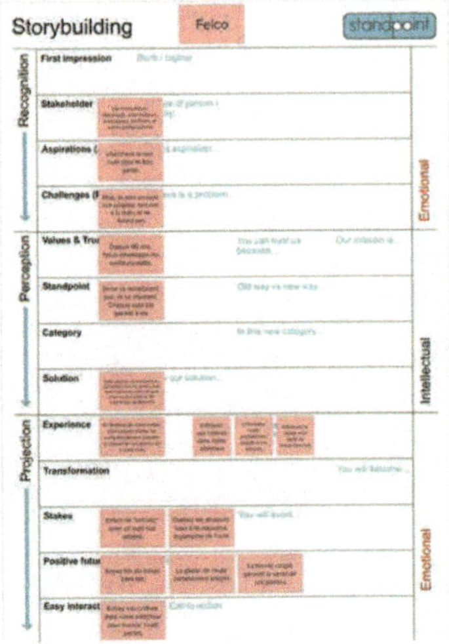

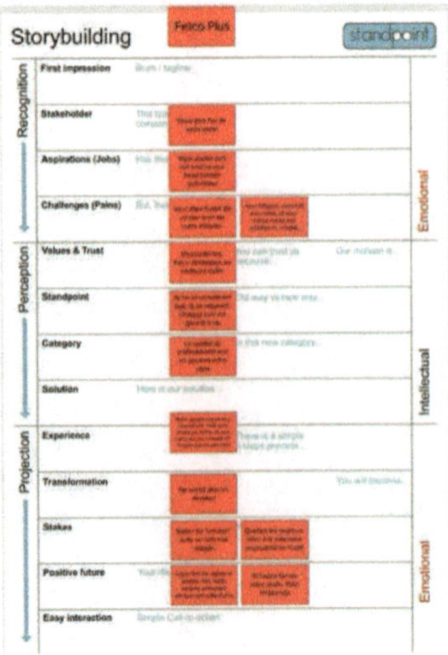

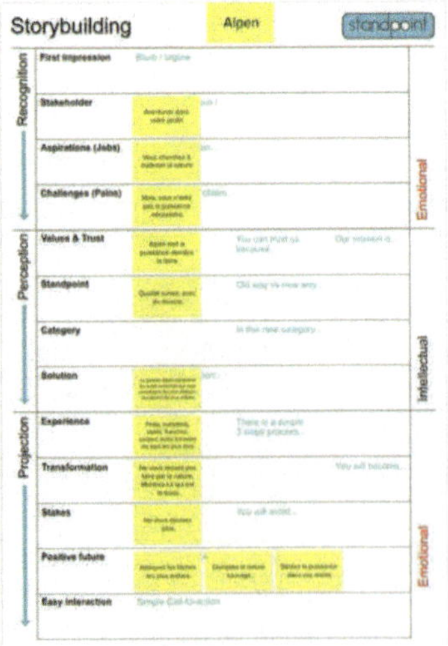

THE OUTCOME: A CLEAR AND COHESIVE BRAND STRATEGY

Felco

With these narratives in place, FELCO achieved several key wins:

- **Distinct brand positioning** for FELCO, FELCO Prosumer, and Alpen.
- **Simplified marketing and sales strategies**, making it easier for distributors to communicate the differences.
- **Stronger customer connection**, with messaging that resonated on both functional and emotional levels.
- **Enhanced storytelling integration** across marketing materials, packaging, and digital platforms.

Each brand now had a **clear, compelling, and distinct voice**, making it easy for customers to recognize which FELCO product was right for them.

LESSONS FOR OTHER BRANDS

This case study highlights a key takeaway: **Customers don't buy products—they buy stories that align with their aspirations and challenges.**

By applying Storybuilding, FELCO transformed a potential branding dilemma into a competitive advantage. Instead of confusing the market, they created three complementary, compelling brand identities that catered to **different audiences, different needs, and different emotional drivers.**

For any company managing multiple brands or sub-brands, the FELCO experience serves as a blueprint for success: **Start with the customer's perspective, define what matters to them, and build a story they want to be part of.**

CUSTOMER CHALLENGES
SOLUTIONS
BENEFITS

B2B-BUSINESS TO BUSINESS

18

It is just as powerful with B2B companies

B2B companies play a different game than B2C. The sales cycles are longer, the decisions are more complex, and the stakes? They can feel massive. But here's the secret: just because B2B is all about logic, data, and ROI doesn't mean emotion takes a backseat. Stories still matter—sometimes even more. They just need a suit and tie.

In this chapter, we'll explore how the Storybuilding method works in a B2B setting. Through real-world examples, we'll show how crafting the right narrative helps businesses build trust, stand out in competitive markets, and create meaningful connections—not just transactions.

The goal? To spark ideas and show what's possible when you tell the right story. Whether you're pitching to a client, forming a partnership, or trying to carve out your space in a crowded industry, this chapter is all about making Storybuilding work for B2B. Because at the end of the day, even the most corporate buyer is still just a human looking for confidence in their decision.

B2B – Business to Business

- IT Support for Co-Working Spaces
- Sustainable Office Supplies for Small Businesses

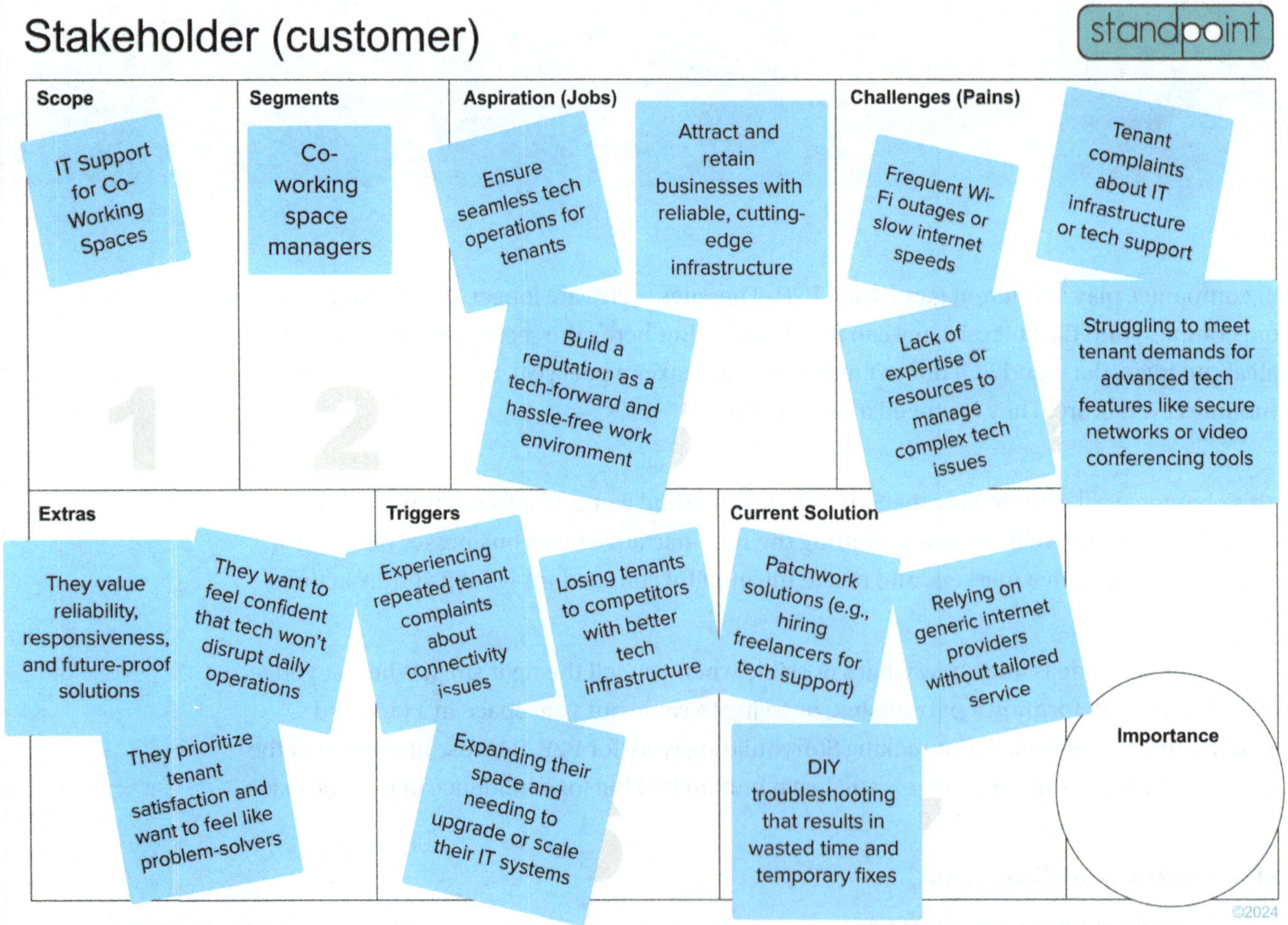
Stakeholder (customer)
standpoint
Scope
IT Support for Co-Working Spaces
Segments
Co-working space managers
Aspiration (Jobs)
Ensure seamless tech operations for tenants
Attract and retain businesses with reliable, cutting-edge infrastructure
Build a reputation as a tech-forward and hassle-free work environment
Challenges (Pains)
Frequent Wi-Fi outages or slow internet speeds
Tenant complaints about IT infrastructure or tech support
Lack of expertise or resources to manage complex tech issues
Struggling to meet tenant demands for advanced tech features like secure networks or video conferencing tools
Extras
They value reliability, responsiveness, and future-proof solutions
They want to feel confident that tech won't disrupt daily operations
They prioritize tenant satisfaction and want to feel like problem-solvers
Triggers
Experiencing repeated tenant complaints about connectivity issues
Losing tenants to competitors with better tech infrastructure
Expanding their space and needing to upgrade or scale their IT systems
Current Solution
Patchwork solutions (e.g., hiring freelancers for tech support)
Relying on generic internet providers without tailored service
DIY troubleshooting that results in wasted time and temporary fixes
Importance
©2024

Organization (company)

standpoint

Enablers

- Identify existing IT issues and propose solutions
- Tailored solutions for different-sized co-working spaces
- Automated alerts for potential tech issues before they impact tenants

Solvers

- Immediate help when tech issues arise
- Improve speed and reliability for shared networks
- Implement secure systems to protect tenant data and privacy

Experience

- Features like automated monitoring and real-time alerts ensure potential issues are addressed before they impact tenants
- Packages are designed to fit the unique needs of different-sized co-working spaces, from small hubs to expansive multi-floor setups
- Always-available assistance

Uniqueness

- Specializes in co-working spaces rather than generic IT services
- Combines personalized service with advanced tech solutions
- Proactively works to prevent issues rather than only responding to them

Brand Persona

- Friendly, tech-savvy, and highly dependable
- A proactive tone emphasizing partnership
- Clean and modern branding with approachable language

Extra Delight

- Regular tenant satisfaction surveys with actionable insights provided to the manager
- "Tech Wellness" dashboard
- Exclusive workshops or webinars for tenants on cybersecurity and digital tools

Matching

©2024

IT Support for Co-Working Spaces

Storybuilding

Recognition (me = stakeholder) **Do I feel welcome?** Do they work with people like me? Do they understand my situation, my problem? **The first phase is emotional.**	**First impression**	**Stakeholder** Co-working space managers responsible for creating seamless work environments for tenants	**Aspirations (Jobs)** Ensure reliable tech operations, attract tenants with cutting-edge infrastructure, and build a reputation as a hassle-free, tech-forward workspace	**Challenges (Pain** Struggling with tenant complaints about slow internet or tech issues, managing IT complexities, and staying competitive with advanced tech features	**Do I recognize myself in this offer?** Am I comfortable to continues my exploration? Yes, I continue No, I give up
Perception (them = organization) **Can I work with them?** What is their standpoint? What do I compare them to? Do I trust them, respect them? Do I understand their solution? **The second phase is more intellectual.**	**Standpoint** Tech infrastructure should be reliable and future-proof. The old way of patchwork solutions is outdated; the new way is proactive and tailored.	**Category** IT support services specializing in co-working spaces	**Values & Trust** On-site audits, proactive monitoring, and custom IT solutions designed for co-working environments	**Solution** 24/7 support, Wi-Fi optimization, and secure systems tailored to the unique demands of shared spaces	**Can I continue with them?** Do I trust them respect them? Do I clearly understand what they offer? Yes, I continue No, I give up
Projection (future me) **What will it be like?** How will I feel? Will I be happy? What will I avoid? What will I gain? **The third phase is emotional again.** Decisions are made more at an emotional level than an intellectual one.	**Experience** Start with an on-site audit, implement tailored solutions, and enjoy proactive monitoring, secure networks, and always-available tech support	**Transformation** Transition from constant tenant complaints to a reputation as a reliable, tech-forward workspace manager	**Stakes** Without this solution, tenant dissatisfaction and tech disruptions will persist, risking revenue and reputation	**Positive future** Imagine a thriving co-working space where tech works seamlessly, tenants are satisfied, and your space stands out as a leader in innovation	**Am I excited with the proposed future?** Is the experience engaging? Does it relieve my pains? Yes, I continue No, I give up

©2024

Storybuilding

standpoint

Recognition	**First impression**		Emotional
	Stakeholder	You're a co-working space manager responsible for creating an environment where businesses thrive, and seamless tech is at the heart of tenant satisfaction.	
	Aspirations (Jobs)	You aspire to offer reliable, cutting-edge tech infrastructure that attracts tenants and builds your reputation as a hassle-free workspace.	
	Challenges (Pains)	But frequent tech issues, tenant complaints, and the complexities of managing IT leave you overwhelmed and struggling to keep up.	
Perception	**Standpoint**	Tech infrastructure should be dependable, future-proof, and tailored to the unique demands of co-working spaces.	Intellectual
	Category	That's why we specialize in IT support for co-working spaces, providing proactive and personalized solutions to keep you ahead of tenant needs.	
	Values & Trust	Our on-site audits and tailored packages ensure your IT systems are optimized, while proactive monitoring tools catch potential issues before they disrupt operations.	
	Solution	With 24/7 support, Wi-Fi optimization, and advanced security systems, we offer everything you need to ensure tenant satisfaction and peace of mind.	
Projection	**Experience**	Start with an on-site audit to assess your needs, implement custom IT solutions, and rely on our proactive monitoring and real-time support to keep everything running smoothly.	Emotional
	Transformation	Imagine earning a reputation as a tech-forward workspace where tenants enjoy uninterrupted connectivity and reliable systems.	
	Stakes	Without this solution, tenant dissatisfaction and tech disruptions will continue to hurt your bottom line and competitive edge.	
	Positive future	Now envision a thriving space where tenants feel supported, tech problems are a thing of the past, and your reputation as a reliable workspace leader is unmatched.	
	Easy interaction		

Tagline ideas

- "Your Tech Partner for Hassle-Free Co-Working."
- "Seamless IT, Satisfied Tenants."
- "Proactive Tech for Productive Spaces."
- "Innovative IT for the Future of Work."

Sustainable Office Supplies for Small Businsses

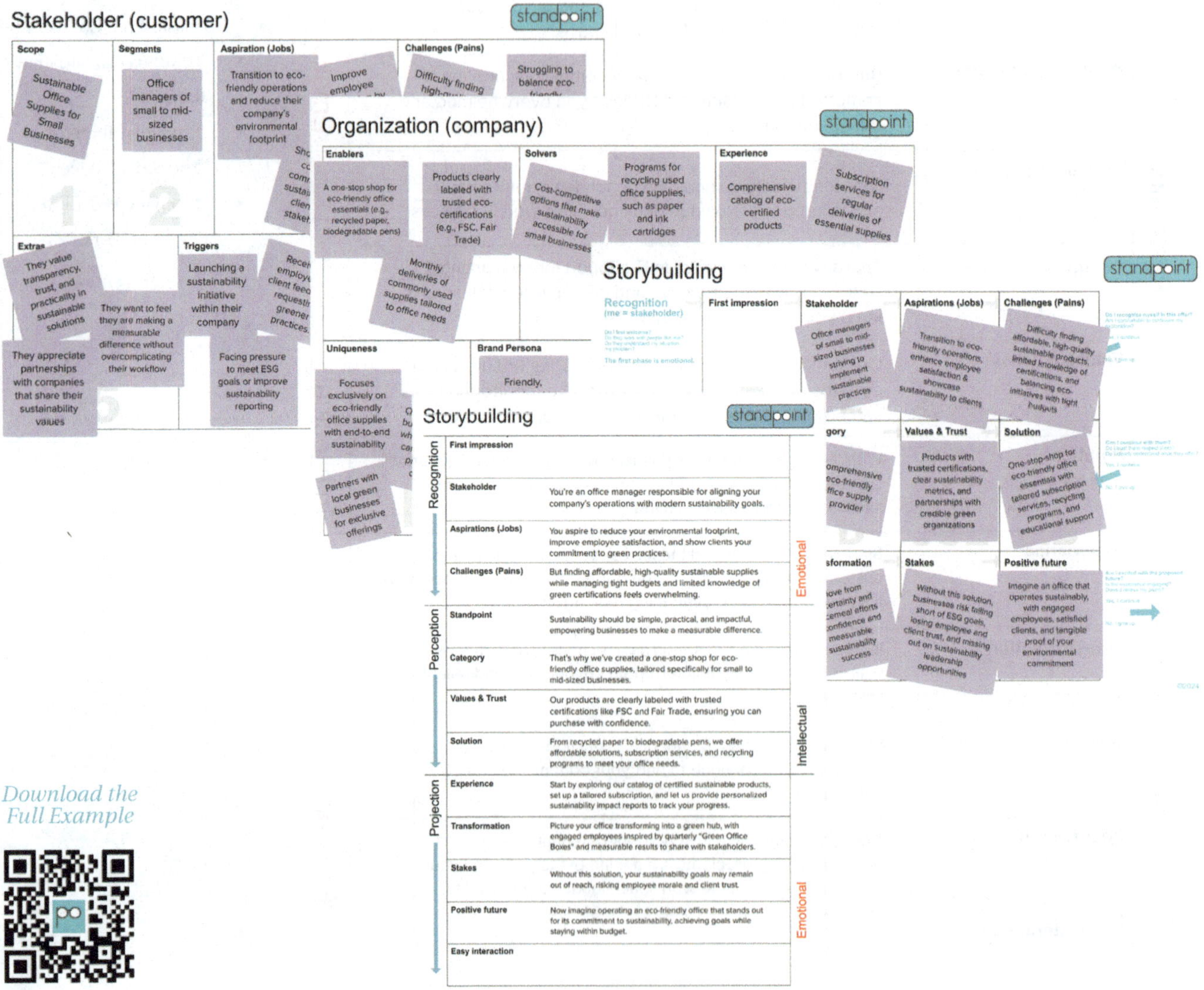

Download the Full Example

B2B Case studies from the Membership site available for download

standpoint

I have worked with numerous companies and startups using the Storybuilding method.

Here are a few short case studies.

- Finbed[1] - Embedded finance
- CertCare[2] – Regulatory Compliance
- fAIcon[3] – AI-powered Conferences
- GoEko[4] – Sustainable Solutions for Businesses

1 Finbed

2 CertCare

3 fAIcon

4 GoEko

VOLUNTEER

NON-PROFIT 19

Non-profits are still "selling" something

Non-profits may not be selling sneakers or software, but they *are* selling something—belief, action, and the feeling that someone's contribution *actually* matters. Whether it's getting donations, recruiting volunteers, or rallying support, the real currency here isn't money—it's *conviction.* And what's the best way to create conviction? A great story.

In this chapter, we'll show how the Storybuilding method can help non-profits craft compelling narratives that tap into people's values, passions, and deep-seated desire to make a difference. Through real-world examples, you'll see how the right story can transform passive supporters into full-fledged champions of your cause.

The goal? To inspire ideas and show how powerful storytelling isn't just helpful—it's essential. Because when people *feel* the impact, they don't just donate. They *believe.*

Non-profit

- Sustainable Urban Living and Community Wellness
- Girls in Tech Empowerment Initiative
- Wildlife Rescue and Rehabilitation

Stakeholder (customer)

standpoint

1. Scope
- Sustainable Urban Living and Community Wellness

2. Segments
- Urban residents, particularly those without access to personal green space

3. Aspiration (Jobs)
- Grow fresh, organic produce
- Foster a sense of community
- Engage in eco-friendly practices

4. Challenges (Pains)
- Lack of affordable access to fresh produce
- Feelings of isolation in dense urban environments
- Limited knowledge of gardening

5. Extras
- Value sustainability and community connection
- Desire to feel empowered and self-sufficient

6. Triggers
- Moving to a new urban area
- Rising food costs
- Awareness of climate change impacts

7. Current Solution
- Buying overpriced produce from grocery stores
- Minimal interaction with neighbors

Importance

©2024

Organization (company)

standpoint

Enablers

- Provide garden plots, seeds, and tools
- Host educational workshops

Solvers

- Address food insecurity by teaching sustainable growing practices
- Build a supportive community network

Experience

- Garden plots, seeds, and tools make urban gardening accessible
- Centralized garden plots foster collaboration
- Educational sessions on sustainable gardening

Uniqueness

- Centralized garden spaces designed for small urban areas
- Free-to-use tools and resources

Brand Persona

- Friendly, down-to-earth, nurturing
- Archetypes: The Caregiver and The Explorer

Extra Delight

- Organize seasonal harvest festivals
- Share surplus produce with local food banks

Matching

©2024

Storybuilding

standpoint

Recognition
(me = stakeholder)

Do I feel welcome?
Do they work with people like me?
Do they understand my situation, my problem?

The first phase is emotional.

Perception
(them = organizat

Can I work with them?
What is their standpoint?
What do I compare them to?
Do I trust them, respect them?
Do I understand their solution?

The second phase is mo intellectual.

Projection
(future me)

What will it be like?
How will I feel? Will I be happy?
What will I avoid? What will I gain?

The third phase is emotio again.
Decisions are made more at an emotional level than an intellectual one.

First impression	**Stakeholder** Urban residents without personal green space	**Aspirations (Jobs)** Grow fresh, organic produce, foster community, and engage in sustainable practices	**Challenges (Pains)** Limited access to affordable fresh produce, isolation in urban areas, and lack of gardening knowledge
Standpoint Everyone deserves the opportunity to grow their own food, connect with their community, and live sustainably. Buying overpriced produce and living in isolation is outdated.	**Category** Urban community garden initiative focused on sustainability and wellness	**Values & Trust** Access to garden plots, tools, seeds, and educational workshops provided by experts	**Solution** Affordable access to gardening resources, workshops, and community events that make urban gardening achievable
Experience Secure a garden plot, attend workshops, and participate in seasonal events while growing your own food and building connections	**Transformation** Transition from feeling disconnected and dependent on stores to empowered, self-sufficient, and community-minded	**Stakes** Without this initiative, urban residents may remain isolated, disconnected from nature, and reliant on expensive produce	**Positive future** Imagine being part of a vibrant community where fresh food, collaboration, and sustainability thrive in harmony

Do I recognize myself in this offer?
Am I comfortable to contirues my exploration?

Yes, I continue

No, I give up

Can I continue with them?
Do I trust them respect them?
Do I clearly understand what they offer?

Yes, I continue

No, I give up

Am I excited with the proposed future?
Is the experience engaging?
Does it relieve my pains?

Yes, I continue

No, I give up

©2024

Storybuilding

standpoint

Recognition	**First impression**		Emotional
	Stakeholder	You're an urban resident living without personal green space, longing for fresh, organic produce and meaningful connections in your community.	
	Aspirations (Jobs)	You aspire to grow your own food, foster a sense of belonging, and contribute to eco-friendly practices.	
	Challenges (Pains)	But the challenges of limited access to affordable produce, isolation, and a lack of gardening knowledge make these goals feel unattainable.	
Perception	**Standpoint**	Everyone deserves the opportunity to grow their own food, connect with neighbors, and live more sustainably, no matter where they live.	Intellectual
	Category	That's why we created an urban community garden initiative focused on making gardening accessible and collaborative for all.	
	Values & Trust	We provide centralized garden plots, free-to-use tools, seeds, and educational workshops to empower urban residents.	
	Solution	By addressing food insecurity and fostering community networks, we help participants grow fresh produce while building lifelong skills.	
Projection	**Experience**	Start by securing your garden plot, accessing tools and seeds, and learning sustainable practices through workshops.	Emotional
	Transformation	Imagine connecting with like-minded neighbors, celebrating harvest festivals, and sharing surplus produce with those in need.	
	Stakes	Without this initiative, urban residents may remain disconnected from their food sources and their community.	
	Positive future	Now imagine a thriving urban space where gardens bloom, friendships flourish, and sustainability becomes a way of life.	
	Easy interaction		

Tagline ideas

- "Grow Together, Thrive Together."
- "Planting Seeds of Community and Sustainability."
- "Fresh Food, Stronger Connections."

Girls in Tech Empowerment Initiative

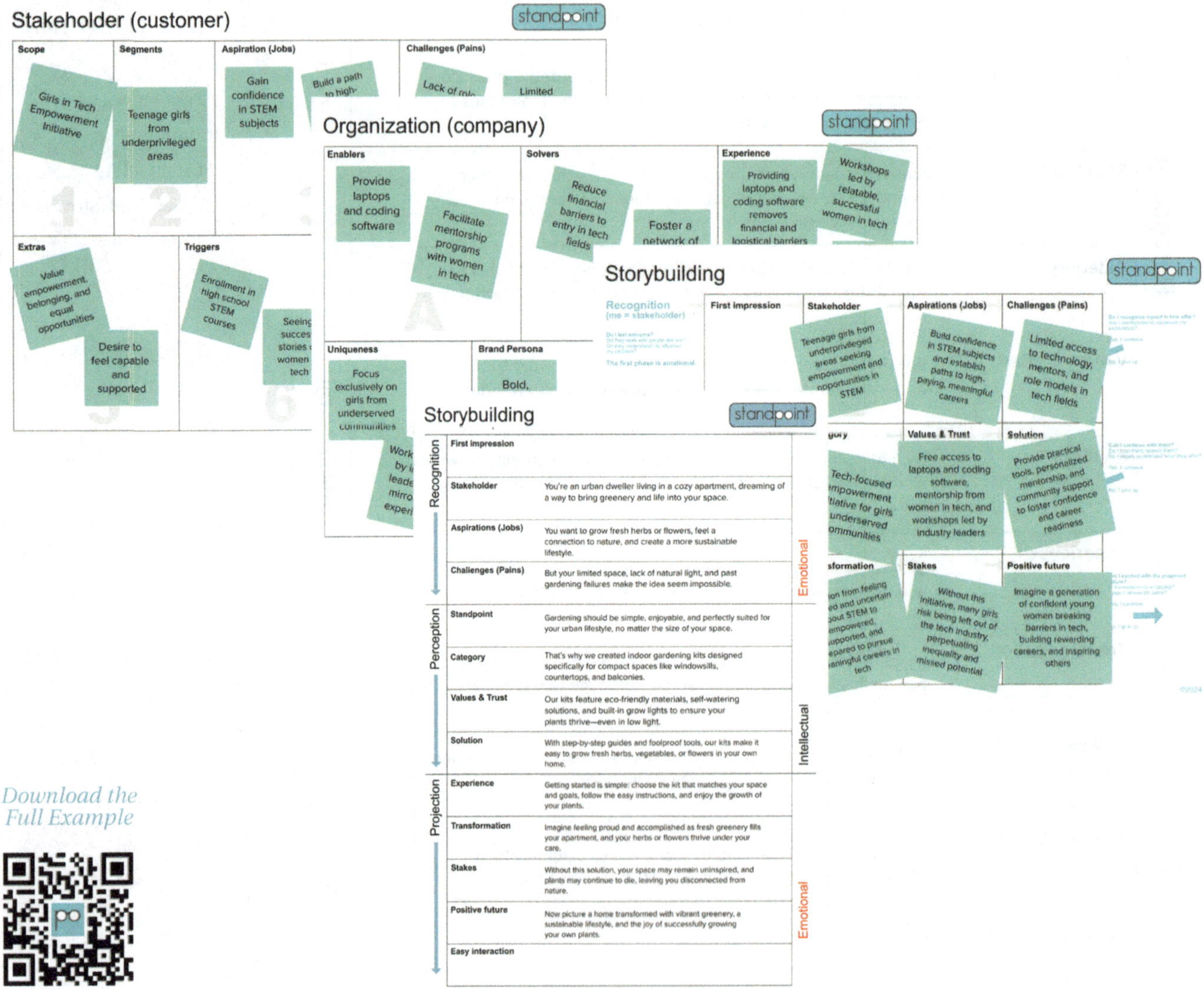

Download the Full Example

Non-Profit: Wildlife Rescue and Rehabilitation (WRR)

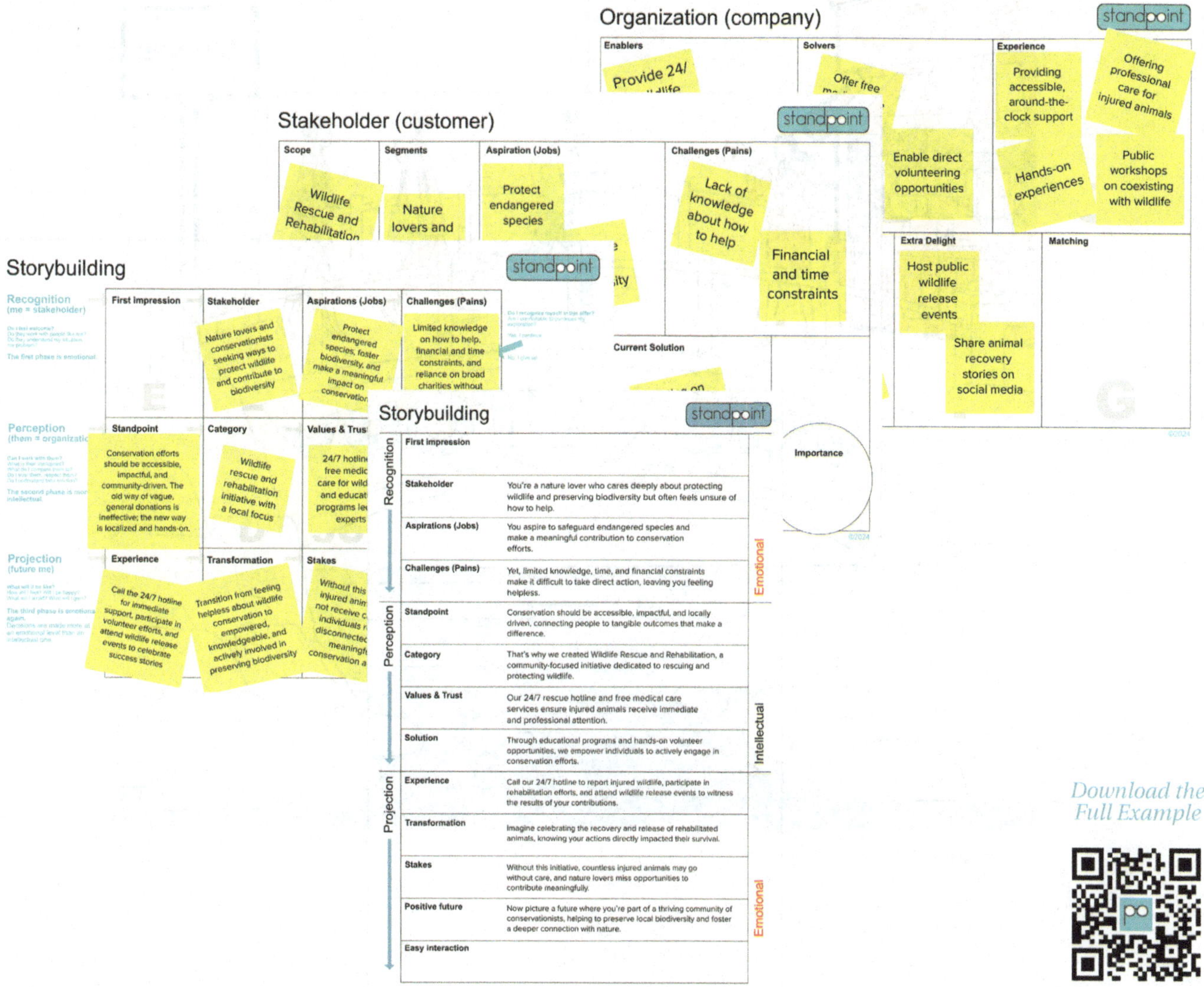

Download the Full Example

SHOP
CLIENTS
YOUR STORY

MARKETPLACE

A little twist when there are two customers

20

Marketplaces are a different beast. Unlike traditional businesses that focus on *one* audience, marketplaces have to juggle *two*—buyers and sellers, hosts and guests, drivers and riders. It's like being a matchmaker, but instead of finding true love, you're creating a system where both sides benefit (and ideally, keep coming back).

This two-sided dynamic makes storytelling trickier, but when done right, it's incredibly powerful. In this chapter, we'll dive into examples of how the Storybuilding method can help marketplace businesses craft compelling narratives that resonate with both sides of their ecosystem.

The goal? To show you how to balance these dual audiences, highlight their needs and aspirations, and position your platform as the perfect meeting point. Because when both sides see the value, *that's* when the magic happens. Let's explore how Storybuilding can bring your marketplace to life.

Marketplace

- Handmade Art & Craft Marketplace
- Peer-to-Peer Rental Marketplace

Handmade Art & Craft Marketplace

Stakeholder (customer) Sellers Buyers

standpoint

Scope

- Handmade Art & Craft Marketplace

Segments

- Sellers (Independent Craftspersons)
- Buyers (Art Enthusiasts and Ethical Shoppers)

Aspiration (Jobs)

Sellers	Buyers
Gain visibility and grow their personal brand	Own unique, meaningful products with a story behind them
Monetize their passion sustainably	Support independent creators and eco-friendly practices
Connect with a niche audience that values craftsmanship	

Challenges (Pains)

Sellers	Buyers
Lack of marketing and technical skills	Finding authentic handmade items in a market flooded with replicas
Difficulty managing payments and logistics	Limited trust in unknown online sellers
Competing with mass-produced goods	Lack of knowledge about artisans' backgrounds or production methods

Extras

Sellers	Buyers
Value authenticity, creativity, and fair trade	Value uniqueness, transparency, and sustainability
Want to feel empowered and appreciated for their work	Want to feel connected to the products they buy and their creators

Triggers

Sellers	Buyers
Completing a new collection or a unique piece	Gift-giving occasions
Receiving positive feedback from local buyers and wanting to expand	Redecorating homes or celebrating personal milestones

Current Solution

Sellers	Buyers
Selling at local markets or small retail shops with limited reach.	Shopping at chain stores
Social media selling with inconsistent results	Shopping at large, impersonal online platforms

Importance

©2024

Organization (company) Sellers Buyers

Enablers

Sellers	Buyers
Simplifies inventory tracking, and order management	Focus on handmade, ujique items with detailed artisan stories
Templates for storytelling, photos, and descriptions	Tools for creating wishlists or receiving tailored recommendations
Metrics on best-performing products	Clear information on eco-certifications and fair-trade practices

Solvers

Sellers	Buyers
Shipping tools with label printing and order tracking	Buyer protection policies for peace of mind
Fast, reliable payments with fraud protection	Guarantees that all items are genuinely handmade
Forums and webinars for skill-building	Customizable gift packaging and direct delivery to recipients

Experience

Sellers	Buyers
Profile pages for sharing the artisan's journey	Updates on support to artisans and their communities
Seasonal highlights, artisan spotlights	Live workshops, Q&A sessions, and virtual studio tours
Tools for creating one-off items, custom orders	Exclusive access to rare and seasonal collections

Uniqueness

Sellers	Buyers
Specifically tailored for artisans	Creator's background and inspiration
Highlight eco-friendly products and practices	Handmade goods only
Access to a worldwide audience	Sustainability and ethical sourcing

Brand Persona

Sellers	Buyers
Warm and Creative	Thoughtful and Creative
Empowering and Supportive	Inclusive and Transparent
Sustainability Advocate	Supportive of Individuality

Extra Delight

Sellers	Buyers
Recognition and rewards for top-performing sellers	Earn rewards for every purchase
Eco-friendly materials offered at reduced rates	Curated lists for holidays or milestones
Opportunities for sellers to collaborate on projects or events	Seamless integration for showcasing purchases

Matching

©2024

Handmade Art & Craft Marketplace

Storybuilding

Sellers | Buyers

Recognition (me = stakeholder)

Do I feel welcome?
Do they work with people like me?
Do they understand my situation, my problem?

The first phase is emotional.

	First impression	Stakeholder	Aspirations (Jobs)	Challenges (Pains)
Sellers		Independent craft creators and artists looking to reach a larger audience	Gain visibility, monetize their passion, and connect with an audience	Lack of marketing skills, difficulty managing payments and logistics
Buyers		Consumers looking for unique, handmade items	Own meaningful products with stories behind them	Difficulty finding authentic handmade items, trusting unknown sellers

Do I recognize myself in this offer?
Am I comfortable to continues my exploration?

Yes, I continue

No, I give up

Perception (them = organization)

Can I work with them?
What is their standpoint?
What do I compare them to?
Do I trust them, respect them?
Do I understand their solution?

The second phase is more intellectual.

	Standpoint	Category	Values & Trust	Solution
Sellers	Selling handcrafted goods should be simple and empowering	Marketplace for handmade, artisanal products	Secure payments, integrated shipping, and marketing tools	A platform for simplified sales, creators' stories, and secure logistics and payments
Buyers	Buying unique, ethical products should be transparent and meaningful	Curated marketplace for handmade, one-of-a-kind products	Artisans' profiles, secure payments, and eco-friendly, fair-trade practices	A platform of genuine handmade goods highlighting the stories of their creators

Can I continue with them?
Do I trust them respect them?
Do I clearly understand what they offer?

Yes, I continue

No, I give up

Projection (future me)

What will it be like?
How will I feel? Will I be happy?
What will I avoid? What will I gain?

The third phase is emotional again.
Decisions are made more at an emotional level than an intellectual one.

	Experience	Transformation	Stakes	Positive future
Sellers	Upload products, share your story, and connect directly with buyers	Transition: struggling to find customers to running a successful creative business	The end of inconsistent sales and burnout from managing logistics on your own	Imagine growing your brand and reaching a global audience
Buyers	Browse artisans' stories, and shop authentic handmade goods	Transition from buying mass-produced goods to owning meaningful products	Don't settle for uninspired, mass-produced items that lack personal connection	Imagine your home filled with unique, handmade treasures that connect you with creators

Am I excited with the proposed future?
Is the experience engaging?
Does it relieve my pains?

Yes, I continue

No, I give up

©2024

Storybuilding Sellers

standpoint

Stage	Element	Content	Mode
Recognition	**First impression**		Emotional
	Stakeholder	You're a craftsperson with a passion for creating unique handmade items, eager to grow your personal brand and reach customers who value your art.	
	Aspirations (Jobs)	You want to monetize your passion, connect with a niche audience, and build a sustainable creative business.	
	Challenges (Pains)	Yet, lack of marketing skills, managing logistics, and competing with mass-produced goods make this feel out of reach.	
Perception	**Standpoint**	Selling your craft should be empowering and simple, enabling you to focus on what you do best.	Intellectual
	Category	That's why we created a marketplace tailored for independent artisans, offering tools and support to grow your brand.	
	Values & Trust	With secure payments, integrated shipping, and marketing tools, you'll feel confident every step of the way.	
	Solution	Upload your products using an easy dashboard, showcase your story, and connect with buyers who value authenticity.	
Projection	**Experience**	You'll gain access to resources like storytelling templates and live workshops to amplify your visibility.	Emotional
	Transformation	Imagine transitioning from local markets to a global audience, recognized for your unique creations.	
	Stakes	Without this, you risk limited reach and inconsistent results.	
	Positive future	Now imagine thriving as a celebrated creator in a global community of artisans.	
	Easy interaction		

Tagline ideas

- "Empowering Creators, One Sale at a Time."
- "Turn Passion into Sustainable Business."
- "Crafted by You, Shared with the World."
- "Your Craft, Your Story, Your Marketplace."

Handmade Art & Craft Marketplace

Tagline ideas

- "Where Every Purchase Tells a Story."
- "Unique Finds, Hand-crafted with Care."
- "Buy Beautiful, Buy Meaningful."
- "Supporting Artisans, One Purchase at a Time."

Storybuilding — Buyers

standpoint

Recognition	**First impression**		Emotional
	Stakeholder	You're a thoughtful shopper searching for unique, handmade items that align with your values.	
	Aspirations (Jobs)	You want to own products with stories behind them and support independent creators while embracing sustainability.	
	Challenges (Pains)	Yet, finding authentic handmade goods and learning about the artisans behind them can feel overwhelming.	
Perception	**Standpoint**	Shopping should be transparent and meaningful, connecting you to the creators behind every piece.	Intellectual
	Category	That's why we created a curated marketplace where every item is one-of-a-kind, and every artisan's story is celebrated.	
	Values & Trust	With secure payments, personalized creator profiles, and eco-friendly practices, you can shop with confidence.	
	Solution	Browse curated collections and learn the stories of the artisans who bring each item to life.	
Projection	**Experience**	You'll discover limited-edition products and enjoy exclusive live workshops with the creators.	Emotional
	Transformation	Imagine transitioning from uninspired purchases to owning items that inspire conversations and reflect your values.	
	Stakes	Without this, you may settle for impersonal, mass-produced goods.	
	Positive future	Now picture a home filled with meaningful treasures that connect you to a community of creators.	
	Easy interaction		

Storybuilding Sellers Buyers

standpoint

Section	Element	Content	Appeal
Recognition	First impression		Emotional
Recognition	Stakeholder	You're either a thoughtful shopper searching for unique, handmade items that align with your values or a passionate craftsperson eager to grow your personal brand and reach customers who appreciate your art.	Emotional
Recognition	Aspirations (Jobs)	As a buyer, you want to own products with meaningful stories behind them, supporting independent creators while embracing sustainability. As a seller, you want to monetize your passion, connect with a niche audience, and build a sustainable creative business.	Emotional
Recognition	Challenges (Pains)	Yet, finding authentic handmade goods and learning about the artisans behind them can feel overwhelming for buyers. For sellers, lack of marketing skills, managing logistics, and competing with mass-produced goods make success feel out of reach.	Emotional
Perception	Standpoint	Shopping and selling should be meaningful and empowering, connecting people to the creators and stories behind every piece.	Intellectual
Perception	Category	That's why we created a curated marketplace where every item is one-of-a-kind, and every artisan's story is celebrated—tailored for conscious buyers and passionate sellers alike.	Intellectual
Perception	Values & Trust	With secure payments, personalized creator profiles, and eco-friendly practices, buyers can shop with confidence. Sellers are supported with integrated shipping, marketing tools, and storytelling resources to help them grow.	Intellectual
Perception	Solution	Buyers can browse curated collections and learn the stories of the artisans who bring each item to life. Sellers can easily upload products, showcase their story, and connect with buyers who value authenticity.	Intellectual
Projection	Experience	Buyers will discover limited-edition products and enjoy exclusive live workshops with the creators. Sellers will gain access to resources like storytelling templates and visibility-boosting tools to amplify their reach.	Emotional
Projection	Transformation	Imagine transitioning from uninspired purchases to owning items that inspire conversations and reflect your values as a buyer. As a seller, imagine transitioning from local markets to a global audience, recognized for your unique creations.	Emotional
Projection	Stakes	Without this marketplace, buyers may settle for impersonal, mass-produced goods, and sellers risk limited reach and inconsistent results.	Emotional
Projection	Positive future	Now, picture a home filled with meaningful treasures that connect you to a community of creators. Sellers can imagine thriving as celebrated artisans in a global network.	Emotional
Projection	Easy interaction		Emotional

Peer-to-Peer Rental Marketplace

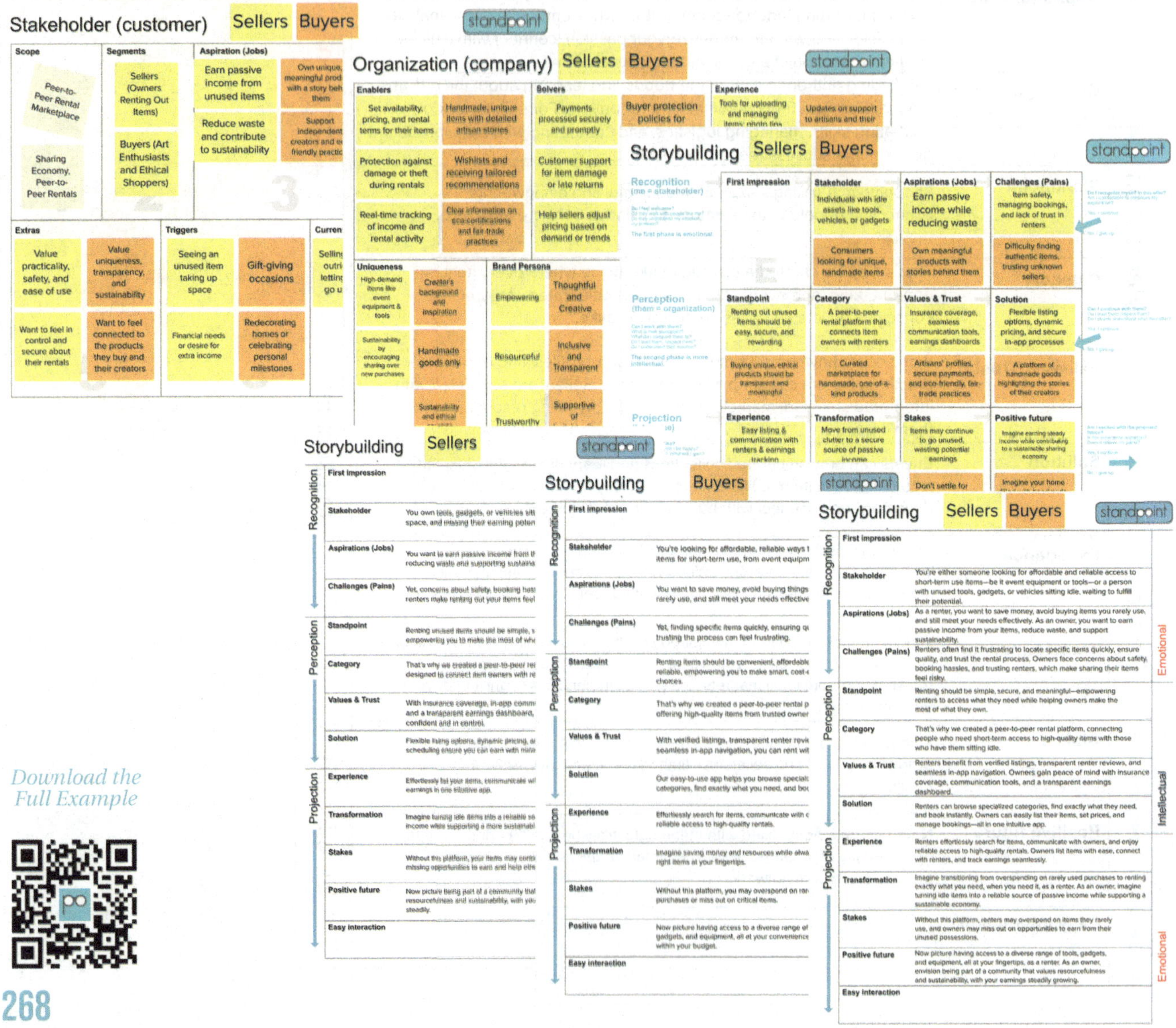

Download the Full Example

VISION FOR
THE FUTURE
OUR
SOLUTION
THE
PROBLEM

INVESTOR

21

You "sell" your idea to an investor

Winning Over Investors: More Than Just Numbers

When pitching to investors, spreadsheets and revenue projections only get you so far. Sure, investors want to see the numbers—but more than that, they want to believe. They need to see the potential, feel the momentum, and trust that *you* are the person who can make it happen. A compelling story doesn't just sell an idea—it turns a pitch into a partnership.

In this chapter, we'll explore how the Storybuilding method can help entrepreneurs craft narratives that inspire confidence, convey potential, and stand out from the endless stream of pitches investors hear. It's not just about presenting facts—it's about shaping a vision that investors *want* to be part of.

Through a real-world example, we'll show how even a deep-tech startup—where complexity can be a hurdle—can use storytelling to position itself as an irresistible opportunity. We'll flip the perspective, treating the startup as the *offer* and the investor as the *customer*, proving that a well-crafted story isn't just for marketing—it's the secret weapon for securing funding.

Because at the end of the day, investors aren't just betting on your business model. They're betting on *your* story. Let's make sure it's one they can't ignore.

Investor

- Deep tech startup looking for funding

Deep Tech Startup Looking For Funding

Stakeholder (customer)

standpoint

Scope
- Deep tech startup looking for funding

Segments
- High-net-worth individuals, venture capitalists, interested in high-risk, high-reward investments in deep tech.

Aspiration (Jobs)
- Generate significant financial returns by backing disruptive innovations
- Be seen as thought leaders in cutting-edge technology
- Support startups that solve critical global challenges
- Build a diverse and future-proof portfolio

Challenges (Pains)
- Difficulty assessing the viability of emerging technologies or understanding technical complexities
- Long timelines for deep tech ROI compared to SaaS or consumer products
- Limited access to ground-breaking startups before competitors
- Risk of backing startups that fail due to poor execution or market fit

Extras
- Values innovation, long-term growth, and exclusivity
- Open to calculated risks but seeks clear evidence of potential success
- Wants to feel confident and visionary in their investment decisions
- Often motivated by both financial gain and societal impact

Triggers
- When identifying an underfunded segment within their portfolio
- Witnessing a competitor successfully invest in a disruptive technology.
- Looking for high-impact solutions aligned with personal or institutional values

Current Solution
- Investing in late-stage startups with proven models, which often yields lower returns
- Passive investing in broad tech funds lacking focus on deep tech.

Importance

©2024

Organization (company)

standpoint

Enablers

- Clear, accessible explanations of complex technologies in layman's terms
- Demonstrated market potential and a strong business case for adoption
- A team of experts with a proven track record in both technology and business

Solvers

- Detailed risk mitigation strategies, such as partnerships with established players or co-investment opportunities
- Evidence of strong IP protection or proprietary advantages
- A roadmap that shows realistic timelines and milestones for product development and market entry

Experience

- Clear, accessible communication breaks down complex technologies into layman's terms
- A realistic timeline with well-defined milestones for product development and market entry
- Real-time updates on technical progress and milestones

Uniqueness

- Focuses on an emerging field with significant first-mover advantages
- Multidisciplinary team blending tech expertise with business acumen
- Exclusive partnerships with leading research institutions or corporations

D

Brand Persona

- Visionary, innovative, and trustworthy
- Balances bold ambition with credibility

E

Extra Delight

- Invitations to thought leadership events featuring industry pioneers
- Exclusive access to early-stage demo days or behind-the-scenes lab tours
- Branded materials highlighting the investor as part of the company's story

atching

G

©2024

Deep Tech Startup Looking For Funding

Storybuilding

standpoint

Recognition
(me = stakeholder)

Do I feel welcome?
Do they work with people like me?
Do they understand my situation, my problem?

The first phase is emotional.

Perception
(them = organization)

Can I work with them?
What is their standpoint?
What do I compare them to?
Do I trust them, respect them?
Do I understand their solution?

The second phase is more intellectual.

Projection
(future me)

What will it be like?
How will I feel? Will I be happy?
What will I avoid? What will I gain?

The third phase is emotional again.
Decisions are made more at an emotional level than an intellectual one.

First impression	**Stakeholder**	**Aspirations (Jobs)**	**Challenges (Pains)**
	High-net-worth individuals, venture capitalists, or funds interested in deep tech investment	Generate significant financial returns, be seen as tech visionaries, support global-impact solutions, and diversify portfolios	Complexity of deep tech, long ROI timelines, and competition for groundbreaking opportunities
Standpoint	**Category**	**Values & Trust**	**Solution**
Investing in deep tech should be bold yet informed, combining visionary thinking with calculated decision-making	A deep tech startup that simplifies access to disruptive innovation	Clear technical explanations, strong business cases & a proven multidisciplinary team	A robust roadmap, risk mitigation strategies, and exclusive opportunities to engage with cutting-edge projects
Experience	**Transformation**	**Stakes**	**Positive future**
Simplified, accessible insights, unique engagement opportunities, and real-time progress updates	Move from feeling uncertain about deep tech to confident in building a future-proof, impactful portfolio	Without this opportunity, investors risk missing out on high-impact innovations and falling behind competitors	Imagine being a key backer of disruptive technologies that solve global challenges and yield significant returns

Do I recognize myself in this offer?
Am I comfortable to continues my exploration?

Yes, I continue

No, I give up

Can I continue with them?
Do I trust them respect them?
Do I clearly understand what they offer?

Yes, I continue

No, I give up

Am I excited with the proposed future?
Is the experience engaging?
Does it relieve my pains?

Yes, I continue

No, I give up

©2024

Storybuilding

standpoint

Recognition	**First impression.**		Emotional
	Stakeholder	You're a high-net-worth individual or venture capitalist seeking groundbreaking investment opportunities in deep tech.	
	Aspirations (Jobs)	You aspire to achieve outsized financial returns, support innovative global solutions, and position yourself as a visionary in cutting-edge technology.	
	Challenges (Pains)	Yet, the complexity of emerging technologies, long ROI timelines, and competition make this space challenging to navigate.	
Perception	**Standpoint**	Investing in deep tech should balance bold ambition with informed decision-making, empowering you to lead in high-stakes innovation.	Intellectual
	Category	That's why we've developed a deep tech startup that connects investors to transformative technologies through clear insights and a well-defined strategy.	
	Values & Trust	With a multidisciplinary team, robust business cases, and exclusive partnerships, we ensure both credibility and first-mover advantage.	
	Solution	Our approach includes simplifying complex ideas, offering unique engagement opportunities, and providing detailed roadmaps for product and market success.	
Projection	**Experience**	Through clear explanations, real-time updates, and access to exclusive events, you'll feel informed and connected throughout your investment journey.	Emotional
	Transformation	Picture yourself as a key backer of innovations solving global challenges, celebrated for supporting transformative technologies.	
	Stakes	Without this opportunity, you risk missing high-impact investments and losing competitive edge in the deep tech arena.	
	Positive future	Now imagine building a future-proof portfolio, advancing global innovation, and achieving outsized financial and societal returns.	
	Easy interaction		

Tagline ideas

- "Invest in Innovation, Empower the Future."
- "Funding Tomorrow's Breakthroughs, Today."
- "Backing Visionaries, Building the Future."
- "Where Bold Investments Meet Big Ideas."

INTERNAL PROJECT PITCH 22

You can also convince your boss of your great idea

Convincing your boss or team to back a new idea can feel like selling a product—except the customers already know all your company's flaws, budgets are tight, and skepticism is practically part of the job description. You're not just asking for approval; you're asking for trust, resources, and a green light in a world of competing priorities.

The secret? A story that doesn't just explain your idea, but makes them *want* to say yes.

In this chapter, we'll explore how the Storybuilding method can turn an internal project pitch from "*just another proposal*" into an opportunity leadership *can't afford* to ignore. Through a real-world example, we'll show how tailoring your message to align with management's goals, pain points, and decision-making process can turn resistance into enthusiasm.

The goal? To help you think creatively about how to position your project in a way that resonates with your audience—whether it's your manager, colleagues, or the executive team. Because at the end of the day, even the best ideas don't sell themselves. But the right story? That can make all the difference.

Internal project pitch

- A Product Manager Pitching a New Productivity App for Remote Teams

A Product Manager Pitching
A New Productivity App for Remote Teams

Stakeholder (customer)

standpoint

Scope

- Product Manager Pitching a New Productivity App for Remote Teams

Segments

- Upper management of a tech company considering investment in new product development

Aspiration (Jobs)

- Drive revenue growth by tapping into the booming remote work market
- Maintain the company's competitive edge with innovative offerings
- Strengthen the company's reputation for solving modern workplace challenges
- Achieve efficient resource allocation by green-lighting the best ideas

Challenges (Pains)

- Limited budgets and the need to prioritize among competing initiatives
- Risk of investing in products that may not achieve market success
- Pressure to deliver quick results while maintaining long-term vision
- Uncertainty in gauging the market potential of new concepts

Extras

- Values measurable results, customer-centric innovation, and market leadership
- Wants to feel reassured that decisions are backed by solid research and a clear ROI path
- Prefers ideas that align with the company's broader strategy and mission

Triggers

- Increasing competition from rivals launching innovative solutions
- Requests from existing customers for tools that support remote productivity
- Shifts in workforce behavior that emphasize remote collaboration

Current Solution

Importance

©2024

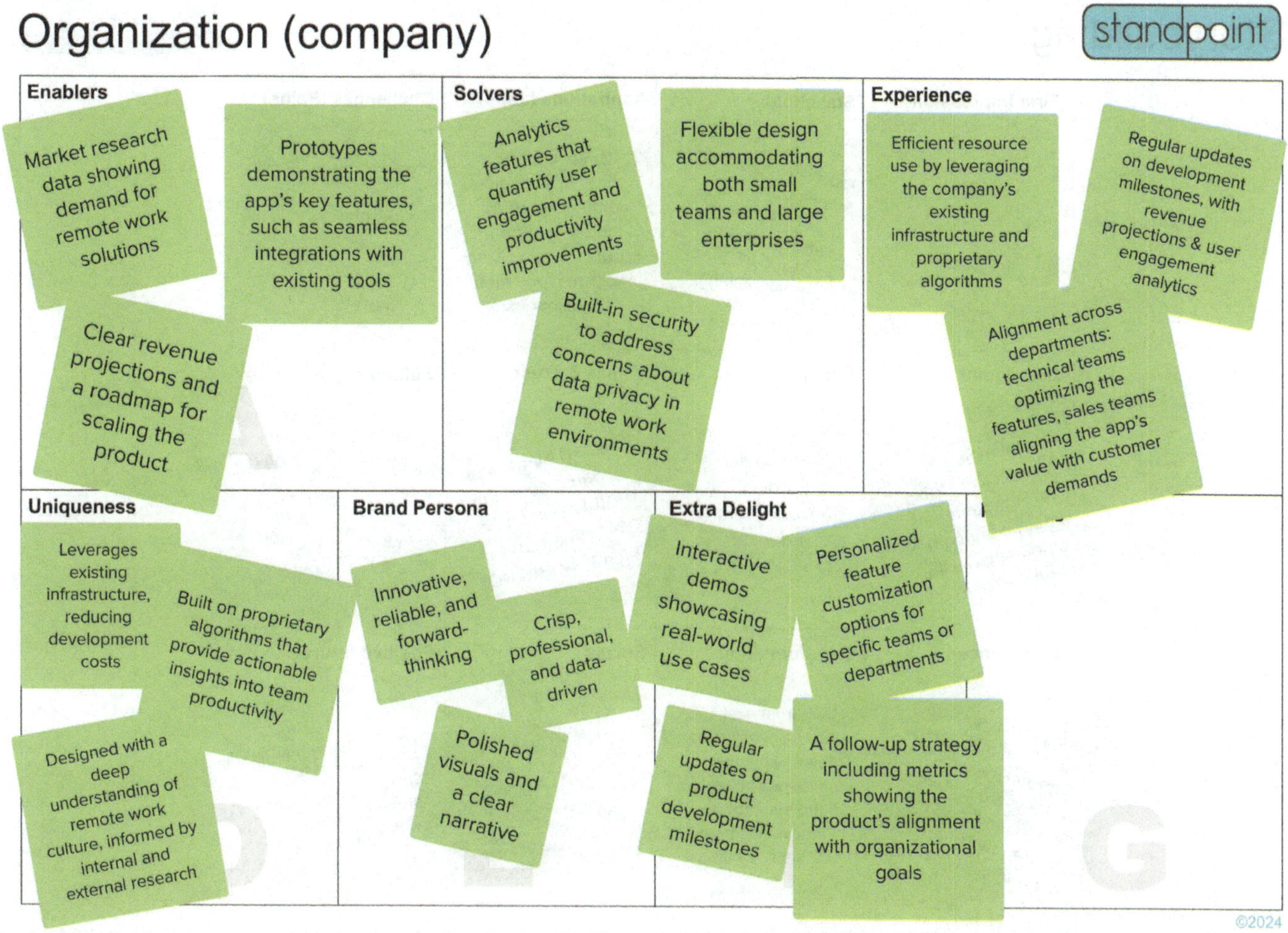
Organization (company)
standpoint
Enablers
Market research data showing demand for remote work solutions
Prototypes demonstrating the app's key features, such as seamless integrations with existing tools
Clear revenue projections and a roadmap for scaling the product
Solvers
Analytics features that quantify user engagement and productivity improvements
Flexible design accommodating both small teams and large enterprises
Built-in security to address concerns about data privacy in remote work environments
Experience
Efficient resource use by leveraging the company's existing infrastructure and proprietary algorithms
Regular updates on development milestones, with revenue projections & user engagement analytics
Alignment across departments: technical teams optimizing the features, sales teams aligning the app's value with customer demands
Uniqueness
Leverages existing infrastructure, reducing development costs
Built on proprietary algorithms that provide actionable insights into team productivity
Designed with a deep understanding of remote work culture, informed by internal and external research
Brand Persona
Innovative, reliable, and forward-thinking
Crisp, professional, and data-driven
Polished visuals and a clear narrative
Extra Delight
Interactive demos showcasing real-world use cases
Personalized feature customization options for specific teams or departments
Regular updates on product development milestones
A follow-up strategy including metrics showing the product's alignment with organizational goals
©2024

A Product Manager Pitching A New Productivity App for Remote Teams

Storybuilding

standpoint

Recognition (me = stakeholder) Do I feel welcome? Do they work with people like me? Do they understand my situation, my problem? The first phase is emotional.	**First impression**	**Stakeholder** Upper management in tech companies considering investment in new product development	**Aspirations (Jobs)** Drive revenue growth, maintain competitive edge, and strengthen reputation by solving modern workplace challenges	**Challenges (Pains)** Limited budgets, competing initiatives, and uncertainty in assessing market potential
Perception (them = organization) Can I work with them? What is their standpoint? What do I compare them to? Do I trust them, respect them? Do I understand their solution? The second phase is more intellectual.	**Standpoint** Investing in productivity tools for remote teams should balance bold innovation with measurable impact	**Category** Actionable product development proposal	**Values & Trust** Backed by market research, working prototypes, and a clear roadmap for scalability and ROI	**Solution** Combines innovative features, seamless integrations, and data-driven insights to meet the evolving needs of remote workforces
Projection (future me) What will it be like? How will I feel? Will I be happy? What will I avoid? What will I gai The third phase is emoti again. Decisions are made more a an emotional level than an intellectual one.	**Experience** Management gets clear updates on milestones, prototypes that demonstrate real-world impact, and tools that drive measurable productivity gains	**Transformation** Move from hesitation about investing in remote work tools to confidence in leading the market with innovative, high-demand solutions	**Stakes** Without this investment, the company risks falling behind competitors and losing relevance in a growing remote work market	**Positive future** Imagine being a leader in the remote work sector, driving customer satisfaction and revenue growth with a best-in-class app

Do I recognize myself in this offer?
Am I comfortable to continues my exploration?
Yes, I continue
No, I give up

Can I continue with them?
Do I trust them respect them?
Do I clearly understand what they offer?
Yes, I continue
No, I give up

Am I excited with the proposed future?
Is the experience engaging?
Does it relieve my pains?
Yes, I continue
No, I give up

©2024

Storybuilding

standpoint

Recognition	**First impression**		Emotional
	Stakeholder	You're part of upper management at a tech company, evaluating new product ideas that could drive revenue and strengthen your competitive edge.	
	Aspirations (Jobs)	You aspire to tap into the booming remote work market while maintaining your company's reputation as a leader in innovation.	
	Challenges (Pains)	Yet, limited budgets, competing initiatives, and market uncertainties make it difficult to prioritize ideas with confidence.	
Perception	**Standpoint**	Investing in remote work solutions should align with your company's mission, delivering both measurable ROI and long-term market leadership.	Intellectual
	Category	That's why I'm pitching a productivity app tailored for remote teams, addressing modern workplace challenges with innovative features.	
	Values & Trust	Backed by market research, working prototypes, and a clear roadmap, this app is designed to reduce development risk while maximizing impact.	
	Solution	With analytics to track productivity improvements, flexible scalability, and built-in security, the app offers a comprehensive solution for remote work.	
Projection	**Experience**	By leveraging the company's infrastructure and algorithms, we'll minimize costs while optimizing innovation, with regular updates to ensure alignment with strategic goals.	Emotional
	Transformation	Picture leading the remote work market with a tool that improves team efficiency, satisfies customer demands, and delivers measurable results.	
	Stakes	Without this investment, the company risks falling behind competitors and losing opportunities to capture a growing market.	
	Positive future	Now imagine our company celebrated as a pioneer in remote work solutions, achieving both customer satisfaction and long-term revenue growth.	
	Easy interaction		

Tagline ideas

- "Our Next Big Move in Productivity Innovation."
- "Seamless Collaboration, Measurable Results."
- "Leading the Future of Remote Productivity."
- "The Productivity App Designed for Remote Success."

PART 6: CONCLUSION

We've built your story, sharpened your message, and reimagined your brand. Now it's time to put it all into action. So, is this goodbye? Not quite—your story is just getting started.

WRAP UP

23

This is what you have learned

Congratulations! You've made it to the end of Storybuilding: *Your Brand From Their Standpoint.*

Buckle your metaphorical seatbelt because we're about to recap the essential points from the journey so far. This chapter is a bit like looking back at your vacation photos—except these snapshots are from the exotic world of storytelling frameworks. Let's revisit, and find out how you can apply this to make your life—and your brand—extraordinary.

THE MAP OF STORYBUILDING

Think of Storybuilding as a three-part treasure map:

1. **Recognition:** Is this brand for me? (Spoiler: First impressions matter, a lot.)
2. **Perception:** Do I understand this brand, and do I trust it? (Think: Does it make sense to you before you commit?)
3. **Projection:** What will my life look like if I say yes? (Ah, the sweet glow of imagining a better future.)

You learned that every decision a customer makes—whether it's buying shoes, donating to a cause, or investing in a startup—travels through these emotional and intellectual checkpoints. Nail these, and you're halfway to being unforgettable.

Part 1: The Encounter

When people meet your brand, they're like someone scanning Tinder profiles: a gut feeling, a swipe left or right. We explored:

- **Recognition:** Customers ask, "Do they work with people like me?" They need to see themselves in your story. Compelling words, and relatable aspirations seal the deal.
- **Perception:** Here comes the nitty-gritty. Customers analyze, "How are they different? Can I trust this? Is the offer clear? Are they credible?" Trust symbols, like glowing testimonials or sleek websites, do wonders.
- **Projection:** The dream stage! Help them imagine the experience and how much better life will be with your brand. Forget logic; go full emotional.

Part 2: Getting Inside Their Heads

Understanding your audience isn't psychic work—it's about stepping into their shoes.

- **Stakeholders (Customers):** We dissected their aspirations (what they want), challenges (what's stopping them), and triggers (what prompts action). Fun fact: Knowing why someone buys a to-do list app or a fancy pen could be the key to owning their wallet.
- **Your Organization:** Look inward, but with outside eyes. What's unique about your offer? Does it align with their desires? Are you the Ruler archetype (organized, dependable) or the Jester (playful, engaging)?

Part 3: Building Stories That Stick

Crafting a story isn't about assembling words—it's about making your audience feel something. A great brand story isn't just heard; it's remembered, repeated, and acted upon.

- **Story Framework:** Use the Storybuilding canvases to map out what your audience wants, the obstacles they face, and how your brand transforms their experience. The strongest stories align seamlessly with your brand identity and promise.
- **Clarity & Resonance:** The best stories cut through the noise with precision. Your messaging should be simple, memorable, and emotionally compelling—so your audience instantly understands why they should care.
- **Customer Perspective First:** Every touchpoint should reinforce the customer's journey, not just your brand's achievements. If your story resonates with their needs, aspirations, and emotions, they'll see themselves in it—and that's when real engagement happens.

HOW TO APPLY STORYBUILDING TODAY

Now that your storytelling toolbox is brimming, let's talk about action. Where can you use these stories? The answer: everywhere.

- **Your Website:** Turn clicks into "I NEED THIS." Lay out Recognition, Perception, and Projection in the perfect sequence.
- **Pitches:** Investors, donors, or team leads—they're all people looking for a great story.
- **Marketing Campaigns:** Nail your ads, newsletters, and social media posts with empathetic insights.

WHY THIS WILL MAKE YOUR LIFE BETTER

When you stop shouting about your product and start telling stories about your customers, magical things happen:

- **More Engagement:** People love hearing about themselves. Make your story theirs.
- **Clarity:** You'll understand your brand better than ever before.
- **Emotional Connection:** You'll go from a fleeting encounter to a brand they remember, like that one vacation you can't stop talking about.

The real joy? Watching your customers recognize themselves in your brand and respond with a resounding, "Yes, this is for me!"

THE BROADER IMPACT OF STORYBUILDING

As we conclude this journey, it's vital to reflect on the transformative impact Storybuilding can have beyond just marketing. By aligning your brand narrative with the aspirations and challenges of your audience, you don't merely create better stories—you reshape how your brand is perceived and how your team operates.

A Stronger Brand Positioning

Storybuilding forces you to take a deep, honest look at your brand's positioning. This process of alignment with your customers' standpoint often reveals gaps, sparks new ideas, and pushes your brand to stand for something clearer and more compelling. Your brand stops being just another option and becomes a confident, differentiated leader in its category. This repositioning isn't just cosmetic; it drives trust and loyalty, helping you stand out in crowded markets.

Team Alignment and Purpose

Perhaps one of the most underappreciated impacts of Storybuilding is its ability to unify your team. By engaging cross-functional teams—marketing, sales, product development, and leadership—you create a shared understanding of who your customers are, what they value, and how the brand can serve them best. This alignment fosters collaboration, reduces friction, and ensures everyone is working toward the same vision. It's no longer about isolated departments working on separate goals; it's about a unified organization rallying behind a common story.

YOUR NEXT STEP

Take what you've learned and build. Start small—a new tagline, a more customer-centric pitch. Test, tweak, and watch the story grow. Just remember storytelling isn't about perfection; it's about connection.

Now it's time to apply these concepts to your brand. The framework is yours; make it work for you.

Author LinkedIn

If you liked this book—at all—**connect with me on LinkedIn**. Should we work together?

THANK YOU

ACKNOWLEDGMENTS 24

Thank you all so much

I am having so much fun, I'm not sure I should be getting paid for it!

I have met so many awesome, interesting people, entrepreneurs, coaches, teachers, consultants, techies, marketers, business types, crazy thinkers, amazing doers, inspiring speakers.

Thank you all.

In my meandrous career path these last years, if I had to pick out one supporter and friend it must be James Miners from Fongit in Geneva. He is my role model for his positive attitude and his unwavering dedication to lifting others up and making beautiful connections.

Thank you, James.

"I want to thank me. I want to thank me for believing in me, I want to thank me for doing all this hard work. I wanna thank me for having no days off. I wanna thank me for never quitting. I wanna thank me for always being a giver and trying to give more than I receive. I wanna thank me for trying to do more right than wrong. I wanna thank me for just being me at all times, John Elbing you a bad motherf**ker."

Stolen from Snoop Dog

standpoint

ABOUT THE AUTHOR 25

John Elbing

Born in the United States and raised in Switzerland, I like to call myself a "structured extrovert"—a mix of American innovation and Swiss precision, with a little improvisation (literally). Years of practicing improv theater in both English and French have certainly helped with the extroverted part.

My "why" is understanding—both gaining it and helping others do the same. I have a knack for making complex ideas accessible… sometimes even to myself.

My academic journey has been as eclectic as my career. I earned a master's degree in computer science from EPFL in Switzerland, but that wasn't quite enough to satisfy my curiosity. At 40, I decided to throw myself back into academia and earned a double MBA in Finance from Carnegie Mellon University and the University of Geneva. That experience taught me many things—including the fact that I have no appreciation for finance.

Standpoint Site

Professionally, I've worn a lot of hats—some fitting better than others. I started in software development, project management, and change management, helping build some of the earliest e-banking solutions. Then, I quit it all to launch a startup. When success proved elusive, I paid the bills by working in digital marketing agencies. That mix of technology, finance, and marketing turned out to be the perfect foundation for coaching startups and companies—especially on *what not to do.*

Determined to "do it right," I built a broad (and arguably obsessive) toolkit, diving deep into Design Thinking, Value Proposition Design, Where To Play, Pitch Coaching, StoryBrand, and Category Design. A mix of all that eventually became **Storybuilding**—my unique approach to Business Storytelling.

As the founder of Standpoint, I help businesses craft powerful, customer-centric narratives through canvas-based workshops. My mantra? *Stop talking about yourself.* (A rule I occasionally forget when discussing my latest projects.) When companies shift their focus to their customers' perspective, they engage more effectively, build stronger relationships, and clarify their positioning in a way that actually sticks.

Over the years, I've worked with over 150 startups and companies, collaborating with Swiss startup incubators and accelerators. I also coach participants of the Executive MBA at the University of Lausanne and teach Entrepreneurship, Business Models, Digital Marketing, and Digital Transformation at various universities and business schools.

Author LinkedIn

Beyond my professional work, I'm committed to social impact. I offer pro bono support to refugees, migrants, and marginalized communities, helping them build their own businesses and create new opportunities.

In short: I love learning, solving problems, telling great stories, and helping others do the same.

I have wonderful relationships with my exceptional daughter, amazing partner and fluffy cat. The cat often seems unimpressed by my accomplishments.

STORY
BUILDING
CANVAS

EPILOGUE 26

Where did this book come from?

Since I started coaching startups and companies, I've been on a bit of a quest - think of me as the Indiana Jones of business canvases. I've tried and tested over 100 methods, tools, and canvases, leaving behind a trail of exhausted markers and enough sticky notes to wallpaper a skyscraper.

One of my trusty companions on this adventure was the **Value Proposition Canvas (VPC)** by Alex Osterwalder and Yves Pigneur of Strategizer.

It was like discovering a treasure map—brilliant at revealing insights. But once the initial excitement wore off, participants often stared at their findings like they'd just opened a treasure chest full of glittering gold… and had no idea which coin to pick up first. Everything seemed important. Where do you start? What do you prioritize? And how do you make sense of it all?

That's when I turned to storytelling. I devoured books on the subject, some of which turned out to be blog posts disguised as books (you know the type: one good idea padded out with a lot of fluff). Eventually, I stumbled across **Building a StoryBrand** by Don Miller. Finally! Here was a framework that made sense. Enthralled, I hopped on a plane to Nashville to get certified. (Yes, I flew halfway across the world to figure out how to tell a good story. Talk about commitment!)

Then came my lightbulb moment: **Why not combine the customer analysis of the VPC with the storytelling magic of StoryBrand?** The result was a game-changer. Suddenly, participants weren't just brainstorming abstract ideas; they were crafting clear, focused stories. And to do that, they had to make tough decisions: What's essential? What's fluff? What's worthy of a starring role, and what gets left on the cutting-room floor?

History

Two unexpected things happened:

The participants were motivated. The goal of creating a usable marketing story gave them a sense of purpose—and a tangible reward: a tool they could immediately use to boost sales.

A Trojan horse effect. While participants thought they were just creating a campaign narrative, they were actually rethinking their customer, their company, their offer, and how they connected. This process often led to profound shifts in positioning—far beyond what they had anticipated.

Seeing this potential, I couldn't stop tinkering. I started tweaking the VPC, rethinking the storytelling framework, and eventually building my own canvases. Soon, I had cobbled together an online whiteboard version where teams could collaborate (read: argue) in real-time. Over dozens of sessions and countless iterations—I think I'm on version 47d now—I refined the method into something truly impactful.

The results? Teams finally had a systematic way to analyze their customers and business, craft a powerful brand positioning, and—bonus!—walk away with a marketing story they could use immediately. No more sticky-note overwhelm. No more treasure chests left unopened.

Eventually, I realized this methodology deserved to be shared more widely, not just with the brave souls I coached one-on-one. And so, this book was born. Inside, you'll find the culmination of my experiments, my insights, and maybe even a few sticky-note scars.

SIGN UP FOR THE EXTRA CONTENT

Flash the QR code to sign up, and start with ***downloading all the canvases****.*

All the Canvases

Secret Reader Access Code

PaleBlueDot

Made in United States
North Haven, CT
10 November 2026

22084530R00176